CARVING REALISTIC BIRDS

A Step-by-Step Manual With Full-Size Patterns

BY H. D. GREEN

Dover Publications, Inc., New York

To Mary

Published in Canada by General Publishing Company,
Ltd., 30 Lesmill Road, Don Mills, Toronto, Ontario.
Published in the United Kingdom by Constable and Com-
pany, Ltd., 10 Orange Street, London WC2H 7EG.

*Carving Realistic Birds: A Step-by-step Manual with Full-
size Patterns* is a new work, first published by Dover Publications, Inc., in New York, in 1977.

International Standard Book Number: 0-486-23484-3
Library of Congress Catalog Card Number: 76-55216

Manufactured in the United States of America
Dover Publications, Inc.
180 Varick Street
New York, N.Y. 10014

CONTENTS

All carvings, photographs and diagrams are by the author unless otherwise noted.

INTRODUCTION

This book has been prepared for the beginning carver who wishes to create the likeness of a bird in wood. With all nature to choose from, what better object to try to duplicate than a bird? The subject matter is vast. In North America alone (which from a birder's standpoint does not include Mexico) there are over 800 models to choose from. Each day offers an opportunity for sighting a different species and potential sculptural form.

To turn the sighted bird into a wood carving requires no great skill. Required instead are a few tools, some good carving wood, patterns from which to carve, as well as patience and time.

After scanning the next several pages you may discover that you already have the first two items—tools and wood. The bulk of this book consists of patterns for your carvings. Possibly the most important aspects, however—time and patience—may be ones that will have to be acquired. For some carvers these can be the most difficult to obtain.

"How long did it take?" is a question often asked at the completion of a carving. Those who ask the question assume there is a correlation between the man-hours spent and the carving's monetary worth. The simple truth is that for even the professional carver attempting to sustain himself by his carving ability, there is no basic formula for equating carving time with monetary return. Rather, a carving should be judged according to such intangibles as craftsmanship and aesthetic value. Its price can only be fixed according to the maximum amount the prospective buyer is willing to pay. For the amateur and especially the novice, the carving can only be valued according to the individual satisfaction that time and patience can produce.

One additional note at the outset: Since you are going to carve them, you should know what birds are. A bird is a warm-blooded, egg-laying vertebrate with its forelimbs modified as wings. Every bird can fly, or if it cannot it's probable that its ancestors did. The capability to fly is not unique. Bats, for example, can fly and there is at least one species of snake that, while it cannot fly, can glide. There is one thing, though, that distinguishes birds from all other creatures—namely, feathers. Feathers are an outgrowth of the bird's skin which provide insulation for its body and substance to its wings.

In simple terms, a bird can be defined as a flying vertebrate, but more specifically, a flying vertebrate clothed with feathers.

Chapter 1

PURCHASING AND USING TOOLS

A basic mistake made by some hobbyists is to purchase a shop full of tools initially, then discover that there are some minimum number that get used all of the time while the remaining tools are needed very seldom, if ever. This chapter has been written for the carver who does not wish to make a large initial tool investment, but rather make his purchases in some logical, practical order. There are many tools that are not mentioned here, particularly powered ones. This is not to say that these omitted tools will never be needed or that their purchase is not practical. Tools such as bench, band and radial arm saws, drill presses, routers, electric sanders, and so on, will ultimately be welcome additions to the shop of every bird carver and will enable him to expedite some of the more time-consuming steps involved in bird carving. However, to acquire such tools can require considerable monetary outlay. Unless you are thinking of bird carving as a means to a livelihood, purchase of these tools may not be justified.

With this in mind, all patterns included within this book have been chosen to enable the hobbyist to produce carvings with relatively inexpensive tools, such as those that follow.

WHITTLING KNIFE

The whittling knife is probably the basic tool for carving, and one that will continually be used no matter what additional tools are later acquired. Many types are available, the most usual being the folding pocket knife. Ideally the blades (which for best results should be two) are of good-quality carbon steel capable of acquiring and maintaining razor sharpness. This type of knife will be adequate for most beginning projects.

The primary advantage to this type of knife is that it can be carried about in one's pocket always available for carving whenever the opportunity arises. The disadvantages as a primary carving knife are many. The blades, because they are folding, have a habit of folding at the wrong time, and cut fingers or split wood can become rather prevalent. Also, the types of cuts that can be made are limited by the size and shape of the blades.

In time, therefore, one may wish to acquire a better knife, possibly a set of chip-carving knives. These knives contain blades of various shapes, sizes and cutting angles. Such knives will give more latitude in the type of carving that can be accomplished. An inexpensive set of X-acto knives will do the job, especially for woods such as pine and basswood. A "whittler's" blade and a No. 11 blade (see Figure 1) are probably the two most frequently used blades. Many additional types of blades exist, as a visit to your local hobby store will show.

A disadvantage to X-acto blades is that they become dull rather fast, especially when used on some of the harder woods. Some people claim X-acto blades can be resharpened, but it may prove to be difficult to replace new-blade sharpness. In addition, side pressure applied during the carving process can result in blade breakage, especially at the tip of the No. 11 blade. The blades can, of course, be replaced rapidly and inexpensively. If your rate of replacement is high, purchase of a more expensive set of chip-carving knives may prove to be more practical. Therefore, it is suggested that you consult a wood-carving catalog for prices and types available.

There are two main points to keep in mind when using the carving knife. The first is always to main-

Figure 1. Typical knives and sharpening stone. Knives (left to right): pocket knife, homemade (barber's razor), manual-training, X-acto (whittling blade), and No. 11 blade.

tain a sharp cutting edge. You will then be able to control the knife better and cut yourself less frequently. Cutting of the stock and yourself, should it occur, will at least be clean, not ripped or ragged. The second point is to keep fingers away from and behind the cutting edge. This is harder than it sounds, since sometimes the better leverage and/or holding position is directly in front of the cutting edge. If this occurs frequently, secure the carving you are working on to something such as a table top, thereby freeing both hands to function in the carving process.

Some carvers recommend that cutting always be done away from the body. This is not always possible. Again, securing the carving to an external source may provide the solution. While this may not keep you from cutting toward yourself, it will make sure that such cuts are better controlled.

GRINDING WHEEL

If you are busily trying out cuts, you will soon discover your knife is dull. You are now left with the choice of sharpening it or buying a new knife. Actually, a combination of these choices is the most desirable solution. Having to stop and sharpen one

knife every time it becomes dull disrupts the carving process. Better to have several knives and devote one time period to sharpening them all. Your kitchen grinding wheel or sharpening stone will do a fair job for your pocket knife. However, if you intend to continue carving to any degree, the kitchen apparatus just won't do the job, especially for some of the additional tools you may ultimately purchase. Now is the time to invest in a decent grinding wheel and sharpening stone.

MAKING YOUR KNIVES

Making your own knives can be fun. If you're lucky, you may find several discarded straightedge razors such as barbers once used (see Figure 1). The steel in these is usually excellent. Barbers in the past several years have gone to replacement-type razors and as a result, the old style may be difficult to come by. In case you can't find any razors, old hacksaw blades of varying lengths between five to ten inches are good substitutes. Grind the end of the blade down to a point and at an angle of your choosing. During the grinding process be sure to insert the blade in a can of water periodically so as not to lose any temper from the steel.

Using the grinding wheel, sharpen the edge as much as possible by holding the cutting edge toward the direction of wheel rotation. Finish by stropping the blade over a whetstone and leather strop. A liberal amount of honing oil should be applied to the stone during this process; this will result in an even keener edge. The handle for your knife may be made from two blocks of wood, one having been recessed to accept the noncutting end of the blade and then glued together. The wood-block handle may be rounded or cut down to a shape best suited to fit your hand.

SANDPAPER

Simple effective tools for getting into the remote and odd-shaped places of your carvings can be made from sandpaper. Merely cut a piece of waste stock to the desired shape and glue a strip of sandpaper to it. If rubber cement is used, the abrasive can then be easily replaced with the same or different grit.

HANDSAWS

The saw you will need at the outset is a coping saw. This saw is sometimes called a "jigsaw," but this terminology is more properly used for the powered version. Although the side and top-view shape of your bird can be whittled down to the proper dimensions, the process can be expedited with the acquisition of this rather inexpensive tool. Blades come with varying numbers of teeth per inch. For pine or basswood, a blade with ten teeth per inch is a good one to start with. Blades may be changed rapidly by loosening the handle. In similar manner, the cutting angle of the blade may be changed to any angle without removal from the stock. As with other saws of this type cutting on the back pull may be more desirable than cutting with forward motion.

Another saw you will find useful to produce carving blocks of the desired size is a combination rip- and crosscut saw. As the name implies, this saw will rip wood with the grain as well as cut across the grain. It will not do either job as well as saws made expressly for each type of cut but it is adequate.

The main thing to remember with all handsaws is to let the saw cut the wood. Forcing the cut by pushing down on the saw makes your body warmer but does not allow the cut to be made any quicker.

Make sure the stock you are cutting is free of nails which, if present, will rapidly dull the teeth of the saw.

VISE

An external device is recommended, as previously mentioned, to hold your carving during the whittling process. You will also need a device to hold your block while sawing it to shape. The vise fulfills both needs as well as several others.

The two basic types of vise are intended for either woodworking or metalworking. The wood vise has wooden jaws and therefore will not mar your work. If only one vise is to be purchased, some prefer the metal because it is more versatile. In this case you can prevent your work's being marred by placing two pieces of scrap stock between the jaws. Some vises can be temporarily clamped to such things as tabletops, while others require fixed mounting. An individual's available space usually dictates the choice of fixed versus temporary mounting. Some models swivel at the base, and this feature is well worth any additional price.

A simple device for holding your carving on top of the vise can be made from scrap stock removed by the coping saw. If that cut was made carefully, this scrap is a mirror image of the top, bottom and two sides of your carving block. This excess stock can be reduced in thickness to approximately one inch and screwed to the end of a board approximately one inch square and six to ten inches long. This board (or jig) may be fixed between the vise jaws at the desired angle, while the carving is temporarily held with two small wood screws to the end containing the scrap stock. This jig permits the vise to be most useful during several phases of bird carving including shaping, feather detailing and painting. The two small holes left in the carving from the wood screws may not be noticeable, but if they are they can easily be filled with wood putty.

FILES AND RASPS

Files are useful particularly during the shaping process of larger birds. The minimum files to be purchased are the half-round rasp for coarse filing and a half-round reaper for smoother filing. Additional shape and size files may be purchased as individual needs arise.

A good device for coarse shaping is surform tools made by Stanley. The cutting surface which looks much the same as a cheese grater can be interchanged with handles to be held and worked as either files or planes (from Stanley Tools Division, New Britain, Conn.).

CHISELS AND MALLET

With the acquisition of a mallet and set of chisels, one begins to cross over from wood whittler to wood carver. Some carvers do not speak of chisels but more properly "wood-carving tools," and one cannot truly be considered a carver unless the chips are made to fly solely from their keen edges. This purest ideology in class distinction possibly originated with the fine cabinetmakers of the Middle Ages whose craft system required years of apprenticeship and work at the journeyman level before one attained the rank of master carver. Articles made by such experts became the possession of kings and nobility, while craftsmen who did not possess such fine carving tools just whittled and hacked out their meager household furnishings with whatever cutting devices were available. It is doubtful that the decoy makers of a century ago (who were probably the forerunners of bird carvers in this country) had such a class distinction. Their main concern was attracting fowl to gun sights and the dinner table. It is safe to assume that the birds couldn't have cared less whether the decoy that was instrumental in getting them there was "whittled" or "carved." For the modern-day beginning bird carver, the point to keep in mind is not to be prodded into the purchase of expensive carving tools when you are capable of producing fine art with nothing more than the whittler's blade.

Even the whittler, however, has times when a set of carving tools provides a very useful and needed function. Getting into nooks and crannies, feather detailing and precise removal of waste stock are examples where use of a chisel is indispensable. A basic carving-tool set consisting of firmer chisel (flat blade), straight gouge (concave cutting edge), and parting tool (V-shaped cutting edge), will get you started. Should you develop a flair in the use of the chisel, you may find it gradually replacing the knife as your basic tool.

As need and skill advance, carving tools with cutting edges of various dimensions and shapes of shafts can be added to the basic set. Do not be alarmed to discover that some manufacturers' tools,

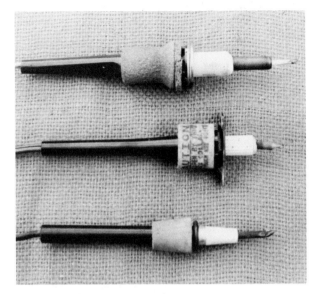

Figure 2. Three types of pyroelectric pens

especially those of fine English steel, do not possess a keen-honed cutting edge when newly acquired. This detail is left for the purchaser to do, and is a skill that must be developed. Holding the tool to the grinding wheel at about a 20-degree angle opposed to the direction of rotation, with frequent dips into a bucket of water, will produce the best results. Additional honing with use of whetstone and strap is much the same as putting a good cutting edge on a knife. The difficult part comes as a result of the shape of the tool. Concave and V-shaped cutting edges can easily be ruined if extreme care is not exercised during the sharpening process. It is not easy to hold bent shafts to the grinding wheel at the right angle. One solution to this dilemma is to locate and utilize a professional sharpening service, especially to perform the grinding. This of course may depend on the number of tools you possess and the frequency with which they are used. When performing the sharpening process yourself, the essential thing as in all phases of bird carving is to take it slow and not be in a hurry. Thus, with time and a few sharp carving tools, you are probably on your way to becoming a master bird carver. In the purest sense, you have now arrived.

DRAW-KNIVES AND SPOKESHAVES

Draw-knives are used by cabinetmakers to shape table legs, handles and other components requiring

Figure 3. Barbs and other feather details may be "burned" with pyroelectric pen.

some degree of curvature. Spokeshaves, as the name implies, were once used by wagon-wheel makers to shave spokes. Both tools have extremely functional uses in the initial shaping of bird bodies, especially larger birds. In principle, they work the same as a carpenter's plane, except the cutting edge is usually brought toward the user. Both hands are required for their use, and because of this, stock to be shaved must be held stationary in a vise. Acquisition of one or both of these tools is recommended for shaping birds the size of full-scale ducks and geese. Draw-knives are especially useful for removing bark from logs.

PYROELECTRIC PEN

This tool (see Figure 2) can be purchased by its full title or simply referred to as a wood burner. As bird carving progresses, so, too, will the desire to incorporate additional realism such as barbs, quills and other feather details. While these details can be produced with a knife or gouge, a simpler means to accomplish this end is with the use of a pyroelectric pen. Two lines which start parallel and ultimately meet produce the quill. Several close continuous strokes of the pen from the quill to feather's edge produce the barbs. Short strokes of the tool over the remaining surfaces of the bird will simulate remaining feathers to provide additional realism (see Figure 3). The intensity of the burning tip may be easily varied by placing a light bulb in series with your burning tool. By simply changing the wattage of the light bulb, you may either increase or decrease the electrical resistance to the tool, thereby producing a "hot" burn versus a "cooler" burn.

A disadvantage to this tool is that, with repeated use, the tip may become disfigured and blunt. The tip may also have a tendency to separate from its housing. These conditions may or may not be the result of improper use. For these reasons, one may consider it more practical to obtain a small soldering iron with interchangeable tips. Some models contain heater elements which may also be interchanged to either lessen or increase burn intensity. Another tool recently introduced to the market is the "hot knife." This tool, because it is a knife blade, will produce a finer line. Unfortunately, the energy element provided is low in wattage, thus making this tool useful for only the softer woods.

With any of these tools, experimentation and practice with several types of scrap wood is highly recommended before one attempts any "bird burning."

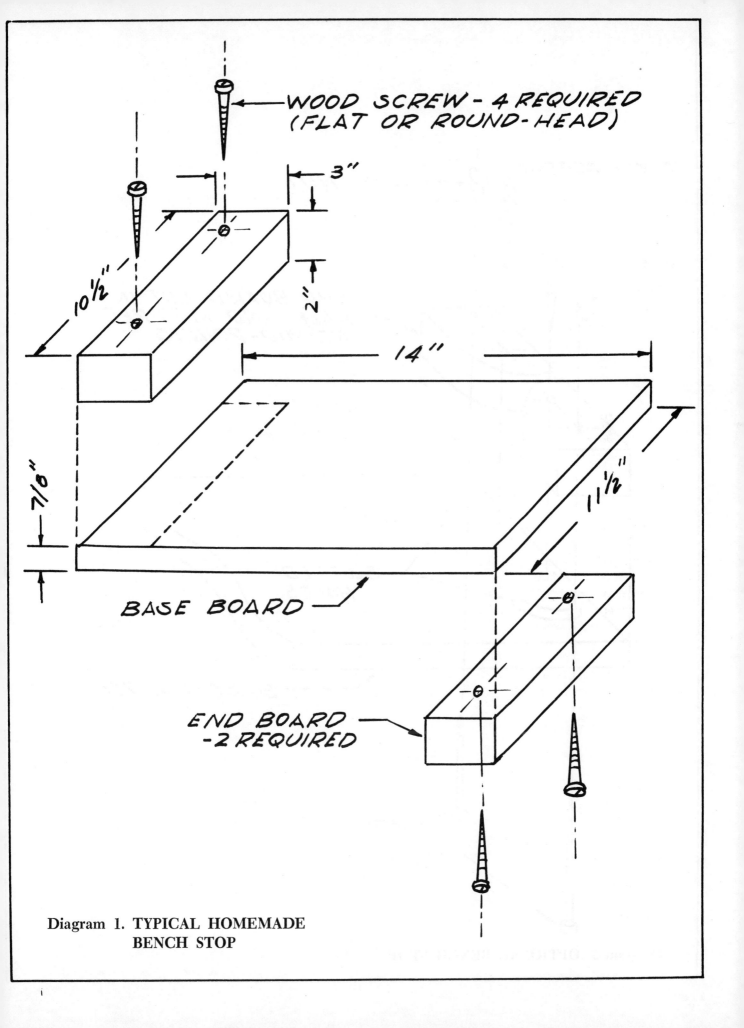

WOOD SCREW – 4 REQUIRED
(FLAT OR ROUND-HEAD)

3"

2"

10½"

14"

11½"

7/8"

BASE BOARD

END BOARD
–2 REQUIRED

Diagram 1. TYPICAL HOMEMADE
BENCH STOP

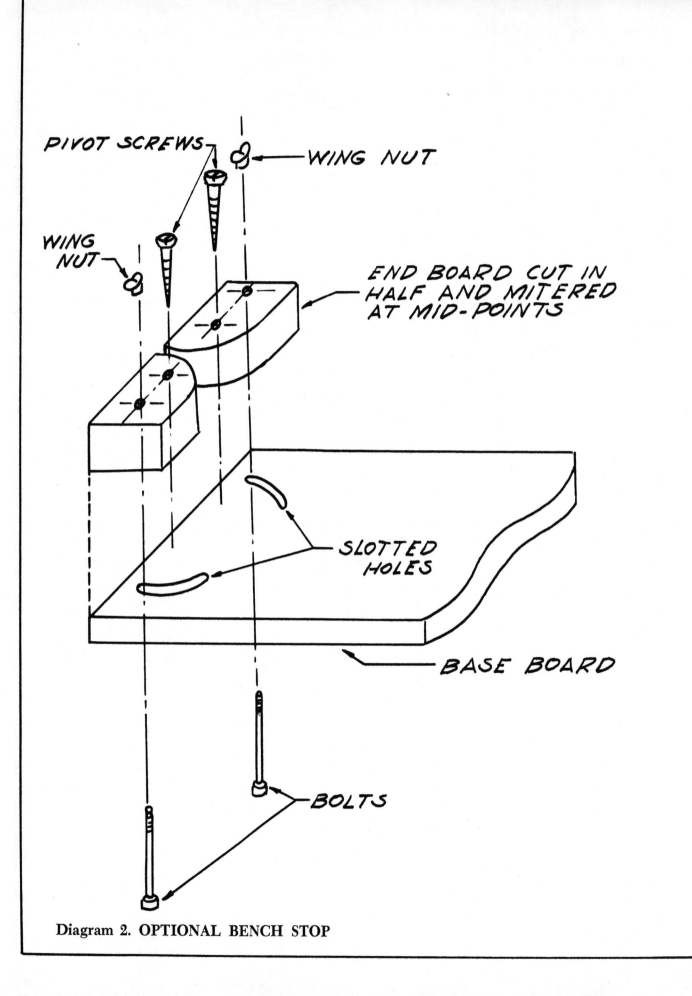

PIVOT SCREWS

WING NUT

WING NUT

END BOARD CUT IN HALF AND MITERED AT MID-POINTS

SLOTTED HOLES

BASE BOARD

BOLTS

Diagram 2. OPTIONAL BENCH STOP

BENCH STOP

A bench stop is a good device to have for bracing stock while it is being cut. Many commercial woodworking benches come equipped with metal stops which are used to hold the ends of boards while the surface is being planed or scraped. Another and equally familiar type of bench stop is the one shown in the pattern, Diagram 1. This stop can be made from scrap lumber to the dimensions shown or to other dimensions which correspond better to the size of material you have available. This device will permit stock to be temporarily held in place while it is being whittled and carved on top of, say, the kitchen table. You will note from the pattern that the end boards are one inch shorter in length than the width or the baseboard. The purpose of this is so that the stop can be used as a brace for crosscutting stock with a handsaw. Right-handers should indent the right-hand side; left-handers the left side.

As an option, the end boards can be cut in half, mitered and secured through slotted holes to the base board with wing nuts. This configuration, as indicated by the modified pattern in Diagram 2, will enable the end boards to pivot from an open position of 180 degrees to a closed position of 90 degrees. Thus the end boards can be adjusted and readily adapted to the end of a square-cornered table. At times, this can be a considerable advantage as it enables one to make cuts which might otherwise not be possible when the stop is limited to side-table use only.

In addition, the adjustable end board will permit stock which is round or oval to be more firmly held in place while it is being worked.

WORKBENCH

The workbench is one additional device that bears mention. Many books on carving and woodworking devote several pages to the various types of benches that can easily and economically be constructed. If you have space and want such a bench (and certainly someday you will), consult your library for books and periodicals which contain such plans. During the interim, all that may be needed is your own lap. As one carver stated, some of his best carving was done while sitting in his favorite chair during the Sunday afternoon TV football game. Most of his watching was in reality listening. For the important plays, there was the instant replay, so not much of the game was lost.

To avoid the annoyance of family-room cleanup of chips or harassment from the one who does the cleaning, some means is needed to keep the waste matter in the carver's lap. A kitchen apron, a shirt with long tail, or sheets of newspaper in your lap are possible solutions.

A better method may be a lap bench. To construct such a bench, first measure the distance between the arms of your favorite chair. Cut a ¾-inch plywood board to a little less than this dimension and to a depth you feel is convenient for holding on your lap. It is important that this board be of the thickness indicated so as to provide rigidity, but be reasonably lightweight. Three sides of optional height should be added to the board, with the fourth or open side facing you. Sides may be hinged to facilitate storage. Add several slotted holes to the board to enable carving blocks to be held in place with C-clamps or bolts containing wing nuts. Drill a hole in one corner of the board and place a removable drawer below it to contain waste material. Further refinements may include an additional drawer for tool storage.

Chapter 2

WOODS

Throughout the world there are over fifty thousand known species of wood. One might assume that each of them is suitable for bird carving; obviously some are better than others. A few of the more common varieties of wood with brief descriptions of their carving qualities are indicated in this chapter. First, however, and especially for the novice carver, there are a few things that should be considered prior to slicing into a piece of carving stock merely because it happens to be handy:

Requirements of the pattern and the degree of your carving ability. You will discover that the pattern you choose should fit your degree of carving ability; similarly, the type of wood should fit the requirements of your pattern. Topknots, crests, long and thin tail feathers, and so on, may better be carved from a hard wood which has been inserted or laminated into the softer wood you might have started with for the body. In addition, for birds which are to remain unpainted, special effects can be obtained by utilizing several woods, each possessing a different hue. The beginner should not assume that the softer the wood, the easier it will be to carve. Balsa is perhaps the softest wood available. Because it is so soft, it is not generally recommended for bird carving. Basswood is classified as a hard wood but is considered by most to be the best wood for both beginner and experienced carver. An inexpensive way to determine which woods are best suited to your needs and abilities is to obtain samples through a wood mail-order house and experiment with them. Knowing the right wood for the right project can only result in a better carving and a reduction of frustration during the process.

The type and size wood readily available. As previously stated, some woods are better for carving than others. Unfortunately local suppliers may not stock the woods that are better for carving. Instead, these woods must be obtained from larger lumber establishments located in major cities. As a result it is possible to pay more for shipping charges than for the wood itself. Woods almost as good, however, may be readily available at less cost in your immediate area. The simple thing to do is to check your supplier, cabinetmaker (for scrap), or other local sources first to determine what is available and its potential to do the job.

The type of finish desired—natural or painted. Birds which are to be painted when completed can be made of blond clear-grained, easier-to-carve woods, such as basswood and pine. Once the bird is painted, no one knows (even you after several years) what wood was used. On the other hand, to paint over a prominently grained hard wood such as walnut or cherry is a waste of what is usually a harder-to-carve, more expensive piece of wood. Thus, birds carved from this type of wood should merely be covered with a protective clear lacquer or varnish. The decision here is obviously one of personal choice.

A minimum list of the more common and popular varieties of wood follows:

BASSWOOD

Probably the best wood for bird carving, basswood is a hard white wood of the Linden family. Due to its unpronounced grain pattern and fine texture, a sharp knife will more readily go where the carver intended it to go. Unfortunately, the wood seems to have little commercial value (the manufacture of toothpicks being one) and usually must be ordered from larger lumber establishments.

Even though shipping charges may be significant, the additional expense can usually be justified by the wood's good carving qualities.

CEDAR

Known for its aromatic fragrance and its ability to repel moths, red cedar is the wood commonly used for clothes chests and closets. Since it is somewhat impervious to weather and rotting, cedar is also a good fencing material. Leftover blocks from a home-improvement project brought about my first use of the wood as a carving media. A soft wood, relatively easy to carve, it has a tendency to split very easily. In addition, it contains an abundance of knots and areas of decayed sapwood which may only be discovered well into the carving process. Because of the applications previously mentioned, cedar can usually be obtained through local suppliers.

CHERRY

A hardwood with attractive grain patterns of yellows, browns, and red, cherry is an ideal carving wood for those who possess tools of quality steel. It is probably better left for the more experienced carver or for those projects where grain pattern is important. The beginner may become familiar with the wood, however, by using it for bases to display finished carvings. Continual sanding and polishing is required to bring out the fine grain pattern.

MAHOGANY

A popular carving wood with color varying from light tan to dark reddish-brown, mahogany is extensively used in the furniture industry, particularly for veneering. There are several varieties of the wood, Honduras and Philippine being the most common. Generally carried in stock by local suppliers but usually only in boards of thicknesses up to one inch, mahogany retails at a price comparable to that of pine. Stock of greater thickness than one inch must be procured from the larger lumber establishments or sometimes can be obtained in scrap sizes from cabinetmakers.

PINE

White, sugar and ponderosa pine are, in the order stated, the varieties to obtain. The one to stay away from is yellow pine, which is usually the one carried in large quantities by the local suppliers. While it can be carved, it is best left for home building and similar industries requiring construction grade material. The carving qualities of white pine are close to those of basswood. Unfortunately, the variety is rather scarce. Sugar and ponderosa pine are good substitutes even though they possess a pitch or oily substance which becomes evident in the carving process. Limited amounts will not deter from carving quality. However, unless a good base coat is applied to carved birds which are to be painted white, it is possible for brownish stains to appear after a few years because the substance starts to bleed. To determine how much of the substance is contained within a block of wood, cut approximately 45 degrees across the grain and allow the block to sit in a warm place for several hours. The oily substance may begin to appear. If only a small amount is visible, the block is probably acceptable for carving. If a considerable amount appears put the block aside for a period of time and try another.

REDWOOD

A softwood with excellent carving qualities, redwood can usually be purchased from the local supplier primarily because of its use as a fencing, decking and home-project material. It is rather light in weight and is usually free of knots. It does, however, have a tendency to split rather easily.

WALNUT

An excellent material to work with, walnut, like cherry, possesses a very attractive grain pattern. Its major drawback as a carving medium is that in recent years it seems to have been sold by the pound rather than by the board foot. Each cut of surplus stock is like throwing away a few ounces of gold. Because of this I suggest that it be left to the hands of the most experienced carver.

Figure 4. *Free wood from neighbor's recently cut willow, ready to be debarked and cured*

Figure 5. *Birch log debarked, with ends sealed, and ready for curing*

FREE WOODS

When your name as a carver begins to flourish throughout your neighborhood you will start receiving offers of "free woods." Free woods include all those noted above, but more probably, the trunks and limbs resulting from tree removal and/or pruning by your neighbors and friends (see Figure 4). Some excellent carving material can be acquired, but you should make sure the limb or trunk isn't full of bugs. With living matter removed, this type of wood is good for ornamental carvings but usually not too good for bird carvings. Should the wood seem solid and sample cuttings impress you as to carving qualities, rent or otherwise obtain a chain saw and cut all logs to varying lengths from one foot to four feet. Strip the bark and paint the ends that have been cut in order to force drying through the sides (see Figure 5). (A liberal amount of white glue applied to the ends also works well as does paraffin such as your grandmother used on her jelly glasses.) Store the logs where air (but not rain)

can circulate about them for at least a year (two would be better), checking and turning them approximately every six months. At the end of the curing time it is possible to have some very fine material from which to cut carving blocks.

In reading this chapter, one may note that missing are ash, birch, maple, oak and rosewood, just to scan the wood alphabet rather hurriedly. Your list may include these woods plus a few more to dent the list of fifty thousand known woods. The thing to remember in bird carving as in all carving is to experiment with as many types and varieties of wood as you possibly can. Although some of the wood you collect may be full of holes, hard to carve, stringy (as is the willow in Figure 4), or even smell bad when cut, at the very worst it will probably work marvelously well in your fireplace. On a cold winter's night this may prove handier than a carving block.

Chapter 3

STEPS IN BIRD CARVING

Let's begin some carving by making three tanagers each somewhat more complex than the one before. To get started you will need:

a. A sharp knife
b. A block of wood—2 inches × 2¼ inches × 6¾ inches
c. Some sandpaper
d. Wire coat hanger
e. Nail punch
f. Piece of tree limb (about 2 inches in diameter or wood block about ¾ inch × 3 inches × 3 inches)
g. Paint—red, black and gray
h. Coping saw and vise desirable, but not mandatory
i. Pattern for first scarlet tanager, Diagram 3

Begin by tracing the "plan view" pattern—the side-view pattern—onto your block of wood (see Figure 6) and cut to shape. This is easily done if you have a coping saw and vise (see Figure 7), but can also be done with a knife—it just takes a little longer. Be sure to cut on the outside of your traced line. When completed, if you are using a coping saw reassemble the block from the pieces you have cut (see Figure 8) and trace the top-view pattern. Cut the block to this shape. If you don't have a coping saw, use your knife to whittle the block to the desired shape checking as you go to the top-view templates which have been traced and cut from cardboard or stiff paper. Completing this, locate the places where the feet of the bird are to go by drilling or punching small holes into the cut-to-shape block, then round the block to the shapes shown at cross-section A, B and C. You will note that a center line scribed with pencil about the block (see Figure 9) will help to keep things symmetrical as your block shaping progresses. Also, remove waste stock from each side of the center line as you go, rather than completing one side before

starting on the other. Sand smooth all surfaces.

When the shaping is completed, cut, bend and insert clothes-hanger wire as feet into the shaped bird and stand. (Instructions about making feet will be given later.) If a tree limb is used for your stand, be sure to cut one side so as to form a level bottom or standing side. Press a nail punch concentrically to either side of the head to indicate eyes.

Next, paint the entire bird red. When dry, paint the wings and tail feathers (top and bottom) and the wire feet black. Also paint four black lines on the stand (see Figure 10) approximately ¼ inch to ⅜ inch long at both points where the wire feet enter the stand. Paint the beak gray. Assemble bird body, feet and stand, thus completing your initial scarlet-tanager carving (see Figures 11–13).

Looking at your finished product, you may decide you could have done better here or there. If so, make another Tanager No. 1 except this time paint the breast, flanks and back yellow. You now have created a western tanager. Other variations might include: all red, summer tanager; all blue with silver-white shoulders, blue-gray tanager.

Now let the project get a little more complicated by making a second tanager (see Diagram 4) with a bit more carved detail. Add to the Materials List two carpet tacks or small flat-head nails (heads about ⅛-in. diameter) and some transparent glue. Complete top- and side-view cutting as before (Fig. 9) and drilling of the small holes where the feet are to go. Next locate the places where the eyes are to go and drill small holes at these places also. You will find it easier to locate the eye holes and make them concentric with one another before rounding the block. With block-rounding complete, transfer the wing and tail patterns onto your block. Starting at the head end, back-cut each feather (see Figure

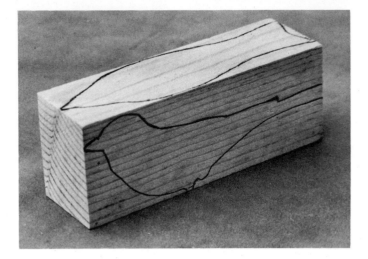

Figure 6. Patterns (plan and top-view) traced onto carving block

Figure 7. Cutting out a carving block for Tanager No. 1

Figure 8. After cutting the block to the plan-view shape, reassemble the block and cut out the top view.

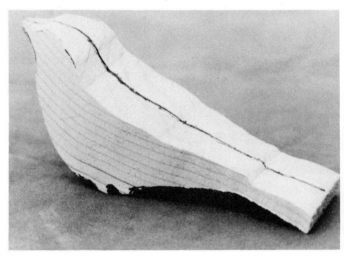

Figure 9. Carving block completed with scribed center line

14) so that it becomes raised 1/32 inch to 1/16 inch above the feather directly behind or below it. This gets a little troublesome, especially on the tail feathers, since you'll want to do it to both top and bottom sides. So, in your initial block cutting and shaping, make this area a little thicker so as to have sufficient stock to work with. Also, you may find it easier to complete feather detailing on the bottom side of the tail feathers before attempting the top (see Figure 15).

Paint everything according to one of the color schedules noted above (see Figure 16). In addition, paint the small nails black and place a drop of transparent glue on top of the heads. Reduce the length of the nail shank to approximately ⅛ inch and insert the nails as eyes into the head of your completed tanager carving.

Let's get still more complicated. You will note that in the previous tanager patterns the beak, wings and tail feathers were all in the same plane. This enabled the bird to be carved from one continuous block of wood. In the next pattern (Diagram 5, Tanager No. 3), the tail is slightly raised, the wings are down, the head is turned and the beak is open. Conceivably, this bird could also be made from one continuous block. If one aligns the wood grain, say, parallel with the wings, it makes the remaining components cross-grained. Attempting to produce thin feathers at the tail thus becomes rather difficult because of the cross grain. The simple thing to do then is to make the bird from three blocks of wood (see Figure 17) glued and doweled together, each possessing the proper grain orientation. Sizes and shapes of the components needed

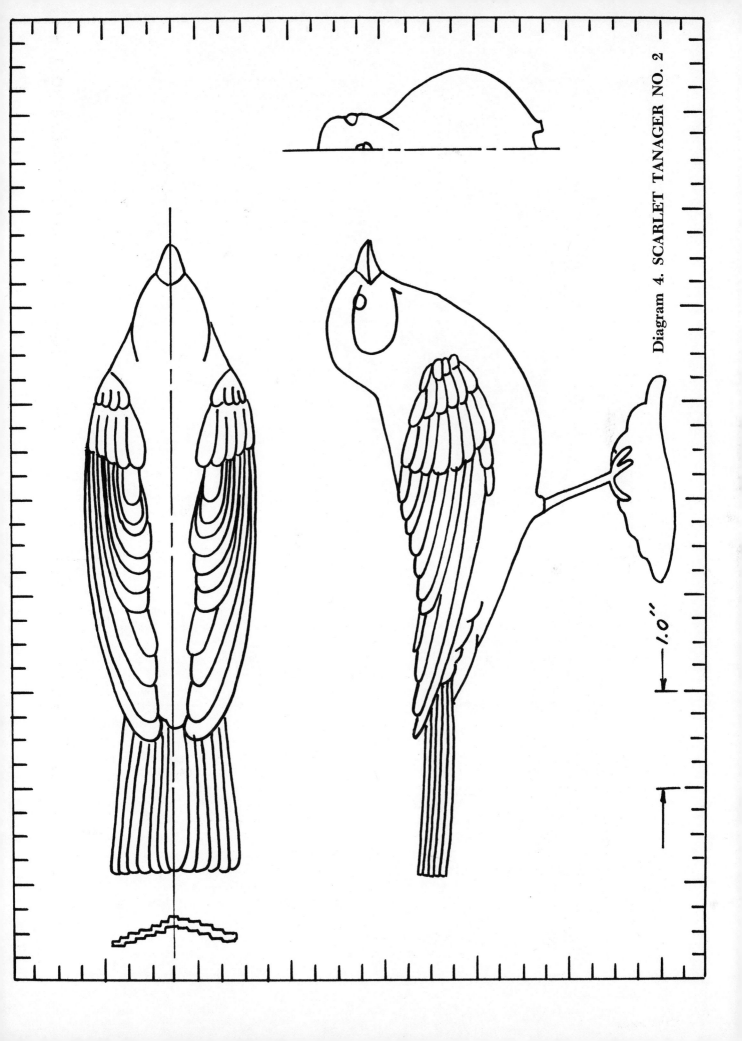

Diagram 4. SCARLET TANAGER NO. 2

1.0"

Figure 16. Completed scarlet tanager

to comprise the laminated blocks are as indicated in the pattern. Be sure clean and smooth cuts are made to the blocks where head joins body. Also, a small wood dowel or pin made from a nail will provide strength at this joint. Shaping and feather detailing are done as previously described (see Figure 18). For added realism obtain a wood-burning tool and burn in barbs on the wing and tail feathers (see Figure 19) with one continuous stroke for each barb. Also, short strokes of the tool over the remaining surfaces will simulate remaining feathers to provide additional realism (see Figures 20–22).

Next, as we indicated before, come the feet. Since you're carving the bird from wood, you might feel that the feet too should be carved from wood. For larger birds, particularly wading birds, feet made of wood which has been internally braced with steel rods make excellent supports (see Figure 23). For smaller birds such as the tanager (as well as the

birds for which patterns are contained in Chapter 8) it is much simpler and certainly less frustrating to try a different approach. You may consider the coat-hanger wire feet previously mentioned to be adequate. A much more realistic-looking foot can, however, be made from several strands of wire wrapped with thread. Two methods are described; the first for birds the size of robins (see Diagram 6), the second, or optional method, for birds the size of finches (see Diagram 6A). Either of these methods will work for your tanager carvings.

For the first method, wire from straightened paper clips and the like can be used but it is better to use piano or music wire, which can be bought in small reels or coils at any hardware store. This is drawn and tempered, hence resilient, stiff and "springy." Wire diameter should be selected so that five pieces are a bit less than the desired foot diameter.

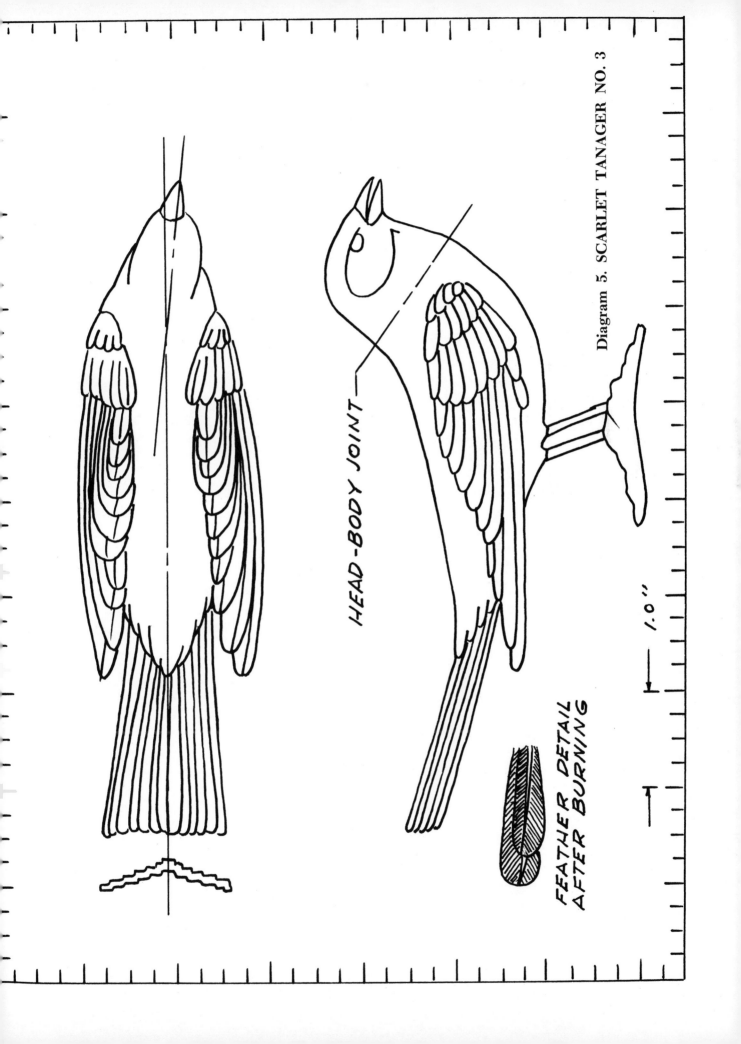

HEAD-BODY JOINT

FEATHER DETAIL
AFTER BURNING

1.0"

Diagram 5. SCARLET TANAGER NO. 3

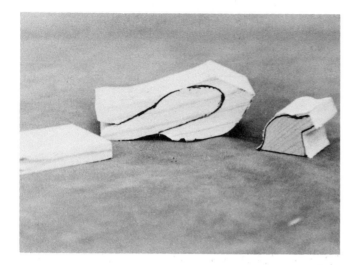

Figure 17. Carving block components for Tanager No. 3

Figure 19. Starting to simulate feather barbs with a wood-burning tool

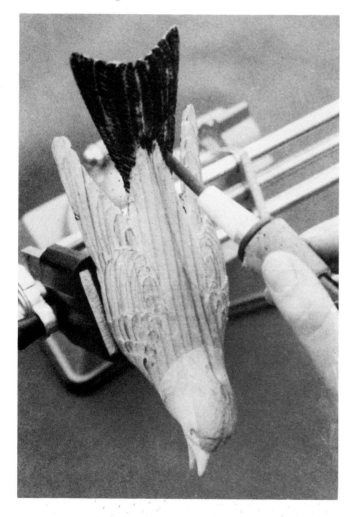

Figure 18. Tanager No. 3 ready for barb detailing with wood burner

Figure 20. Western tanager

Measure the length of the bird's middle toe, foot and body depth from the pattern. Cut eight pieces of wire to this total length and sharpen one end of each into a claw tip with file or grinder.

Next, measure the length of each toe and claw and bend the wires at the sharpened end at about 30 degrees for each. (You'll note that each "toe" varies in length, the middle one being the longest.)

Cut two more pieces of wire, each a few inches longer than the original eight. Use one of these longer wires as a core and group a set of the four bent wires around it with the toes in approximately the proper positions. Wrap a piece of tape around the assembly of strands. Do the same with the other set.

Drill holes at proper locations in the bird's body to take the bundle of five wires and drill holes in the stand to take the central, longer one. Assemble bird, feet and stand, bending feet and toes as necessary to provide proper orientation, especially toes

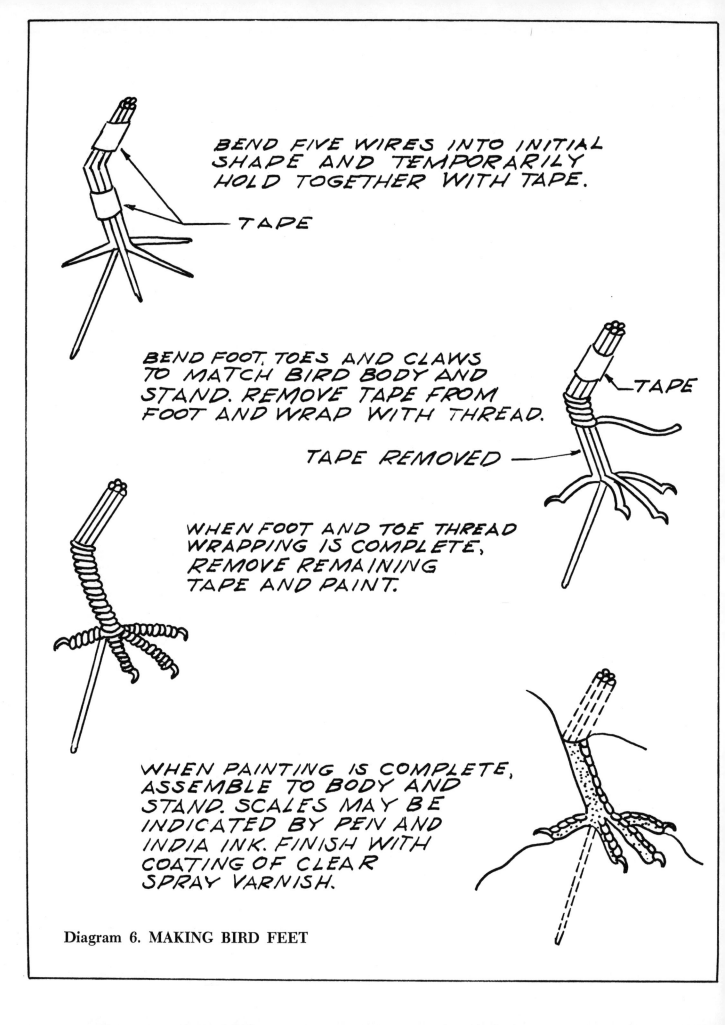

BEND FIVE WIRES INTO INITIAL SHAPE AND TEMPORARILY HOLD TOGETHER WITH TAPE.

TAPE

BEND FOOT, TOES AND CLAWS TO MATCH BIRD BODY AND STAND. REMOVE TAPE FROM FOOT AND WRAP WITH THREAD.

TAPE

TAPE REMOVED

WHEN FOOT AND TOE THREAD WRAPPING IS COMPLETE, REMOVE REMAINING TAPE AND PAINT.

WHEN PAINTING IS COMPLETE, ASSEMBLE TO BODY AND STAND. SCALES MAY BE INDICATED BY PEN AND INDIA INK. FINISH WITH COATING OF CLEAR SPRAY VARNISH.

Diagram 6. MAKING BIRD FEET

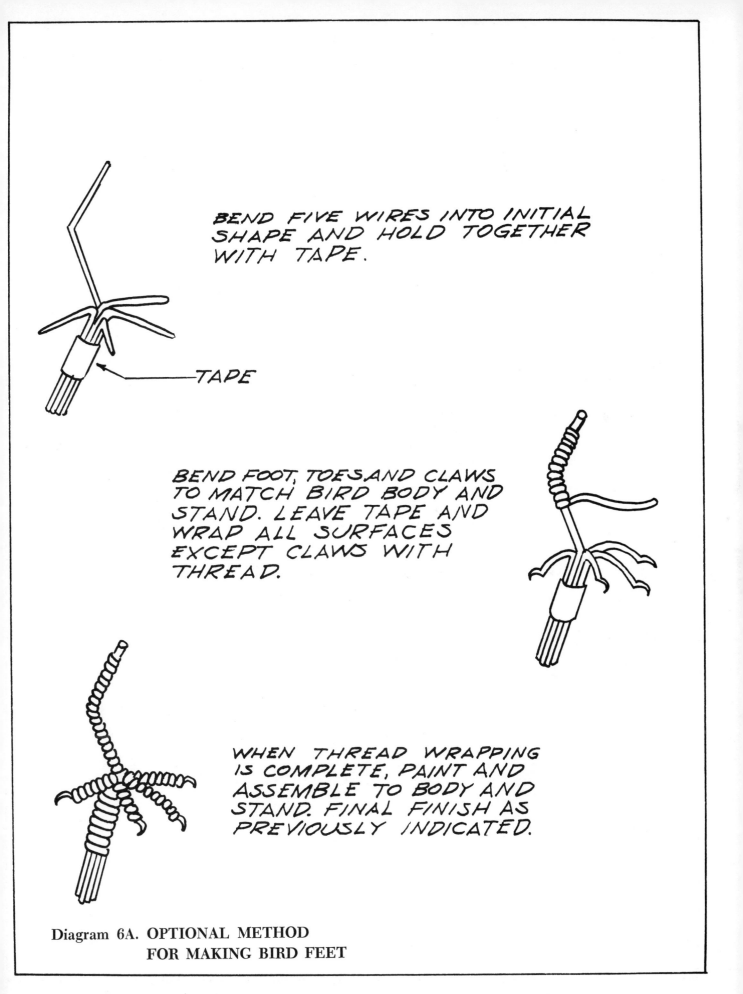

BEND FIVE WIRES INTO INITIAL
SHAPE AND HOLD TOGETHER
WITH TAPE.

—TAPE

BEND FOOT, TOES AND CLAWS
TO MATCH BIRD BODY AND
STAND. LEAVE TAPE AND
WRAP ALL SURFACES
EXCEPT CLAWS WITH
THREAD.

WHEN THREAD WRAPPING
IS COMPLETE, PAINT AND
ASSEMBLE TO BODY AND
STAND. FINAL FINISH AS
PREVIOUSLY INDICATED.

Diagram 6A. OPTIONAL METHOD
         FOR MAKING BIRD FEET

Figure 21. Male (top) and female Western tanagers

at points where they contact the stand. Remove the feet from bird and stand.

Wrap all surfaces with thread except those that go into the body and stand and the eight claws, removing the tape to clear the thread as you work. Several twists of thread about the toes may be necessary to obtain proper thickness, but only one should be required about the feet. Thread ends can be held with glue.

For the second, or optional method, cut two pieces of music wire of sufficient length to include the foot dimension plus an inch or so at either end to be inserted into the bird's body and the stand respectively. Cut eight more pieces of wire the required length of the toes and claws plus an additional inch or so for each. It is not necessary that the "toe" wire be music wire, and in fact for very small birds, fine strands of copper wire works well. Group a set of four shorter wires at the end of one of the longer wires and wrap a piece of tape around the assembly of strands. Do the same with the other set. Assemble bird, feet and stand (taped wires go into the strand), bending feet and toes as necessary to provide proper orientation, especially toes at points where they contact the stand. Remove the feet from the bird and stand and wrap all surfaces of the wire with thread except the eight claws.

The primary advantage to this procedure over that previously described is that it produces a foot of much smaller diameter, which is, of course, necessary for a smaller bird. One additional feature you will discover after the mounting is complete—the bird may tend to vibrate or "quiver" whenever there is a slight draft or jarring of the stand. As a result, the bird will almost look alive.

Using either of these procedures, the feet can now be painted and assembled. They should have a final coat of luster varnish to produce the proper sheen.

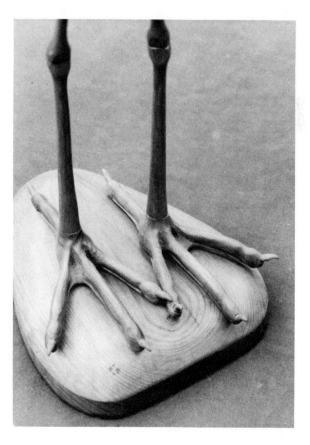

Figure 22. Bottom side of Western tanager. The third tanager pattern was used as a basis; wings were opened beyond that indicated in pattern but carved as integral part of body block. Alternative procedure: carve each wing separately, attach them to body before painting.

Figure 23. Carved feet of a wading bird

Chapter 4

BIRD COLORATION AND PAINTING

Although the emphasis in this book in on bird carving, this book would not be complete unless something was included about bird coloration and painting. For some species the only means to differentiate one from another readily is by coloration. The tanager as decribed in Chapter 3 is a good example. Perhaps not the only but certainly the easiest way to distinguish a scarlet from a western or a summer tanager is by coloration. For some carvers this may be carried a step further, if they rely more on their paintbrush for details than their carving tools. Admittedly an intricately painted wooden bird containing no detailed carving can be most attractive, more so if you have ever priced one. While one should not criticize this type of creative work, one may wonder at what point it ceases to be bird carving and becomes three-dimensional bird painting. Obviously, there must be some middle ground between bird carving and bird painting, but where it is each reader must decide; in the meantime we will proceed with the subject of bird coloration and painting.

Simply stated, a bird's coloration is usually due to pigment or structure, and what the human eye perceives is a combination of both. Pigment is the result of the chemical makeup, while structure is the result of the physical makeup. Hold a yellow feather up to a light source and it will appear yellow simply because its pigment or chemistry makes it so. Hold a blue feather in similar fashion and it will appear brown as there are no known blue pigments in birds. What the human eye originally perceived to be blue, as in the blue jay, was strictly the result of the structure or physical makeup of each feather. This is not meant to suggest that you paint the blue jay brown, but rather to indicate that by changing the angle or source of light, so too will

there be a change in color. This is particularly true of iridescent colors similar to those in a soap bubble. The common grackle, for example, is seemingly black. Vary the light source and reflections will go from reds to violets to blues and to greens. To give an accurate color description of a rubythroat hummingbird, the observer must almost specify whether the light source was behind or in front of it.

The color of some birds, particularly males, will also vary according to the season. Male cardinals in fresh molt are quite grayish, especially on their back. Not until late spring is the cardinal bright red.

Migratory birds may change color according to the food available to them within their temporary locale. A predominantly yellow bird may begin to appear orange after a continued diet of red berries. The American avocet does not assume the rust neck and head until it begins to leave its South Texas winter home. The gray of a Texas scissortailed flycatcher will be different from the gray of its Oklahoma relative.

Thus we may begin to realize some of the problems and challenges associated with attempts to duplicate the true color of a bird. One's best effort will usually fall short and we haven't even begun to consider such things as luster and sheen. To be capable of producing a really good, painted bird carving requires not only carving skill but also a sound knowledge of bird coloration and skill in duplicating color. Many excellent books addressed to the mixing and application of various mediums such as oils and acrylics are available. Art courses are offered in most localities for all levels of skill. Both the books and the courses will be helpful in providing a solid foundation for the carver who has not yet done very much painting. The problem is that both art book and course will be couched in terms of how to make a two-dimensional surface look as if it were three-dimensional. For bird painting, what is required is almost the reverse. The bird carver needs to learn the technique of starting with a three-dimensional object and applying color almost in two-dimensional fashion. This is a skill that can only be acquired through practice and experience.

Probably the most widely used mediums for carved bird painting are those previously mentioned —oils and acrylics. Both have their advantages and disadvantages. Oils take a long time to dry and this can be annoying when you are painting a bird whose belly is one color, his back another, and his head still a third. On the other hand, oils blend nicely, can be used to create texture, and when dry will tend to produce the proper sheen. Acrylics dry fast—in fact, almost too fast. This problem can be overcome with the addition of acrylic retarding medium mixed into the paint as it comes out of the tube. Frequently the finish may be too shiny, especially if several layers of paint have been applied. The sheen can be reduced, however, by applying a matte finish as a final coat. The amount of sheen can also be reduced by adding water to the paint in lieu of the drying agent during the painting process. Means for applying the paint include brushes of various widths and bristle stiffness or an airbrush.

Special effects such as vermiculations can be accomplished with India ink or felt-tip pen. These substances will rub off rather easily, even after they have been allowed to dry for several hours. Thus it will be necessary to apply a clear matte spray over the ink as a final finish.

Possibly the most difficult finish to produce is iridescence. Some degree of success can be obtained by arbitrarily establishing the proper light source for viewing, say, either side and to the rear of the bird's upper body, then blending in various shades of violet, blue and green. This technique will work well on a bird such as a purple martin. If you created feather barbs with a pyroelectric pen as previously described, the iridescent illusion may be attained with the use of colored pencils. For a black bird, e.g., lightly scribe a line on one side of each barb with a red pencil and to the other side of each barb with a yellow pencil. The red pencil over the black-base coat will appear violet whereas the yellow pencil will appear green. When completed, apply a combination of luster-clear spray varnish and as necessary, clear spray matte finish, having first made sure the two spray finishes are compatible. When dry, keep the light source constant and as you move your head up and down or from side to side, some degree of iridescence will seem to be visible.

You will soon find that a good file of colored pictures will be imperative. Bird paintings will be helpful, but one should remember that the painter is trying to transform a two-dimensional surface into a three-dimensional illusion, and his accuracy in bird coloration may therefore be deceptive, especially in shadowed areas. For this reason, photographs may prove better, but they too will be dependent upon lighting conditions. It is interesting to note how the reds of a cardinal will vary from painting to painting or from photograph to photograph. Stuffed birds are also useful as models, but the feathers tend to lose some of their natural luster with age. Field observation is perhaps the best method for determining true coloration, but it too has its drawbacks. For one thing it is not always possible and secondly, when it is, the bird won't cooperate by staying long enough for you to get a good glimpse. What is required is a combination of all procedures mentioned, plus practice and patience—trial and error.

With time, you will hopefully be successful in developing and combining both talents of bird carving and bird painting. As a result, you will have achieved that middle ground, and no one including yourself will question whether your work is a carved bird or a painted bird. Rather it will be obvious to all that it is a culmination derived from both artistic worlds.

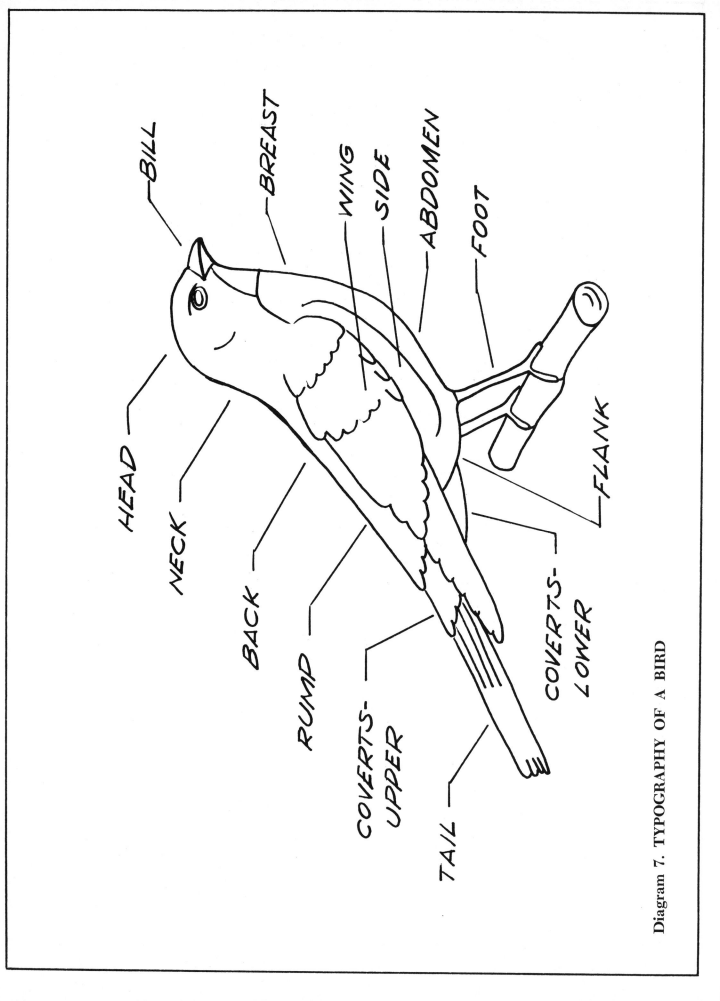

Diagram 7. TYPOGRAPHY OF A BIRD

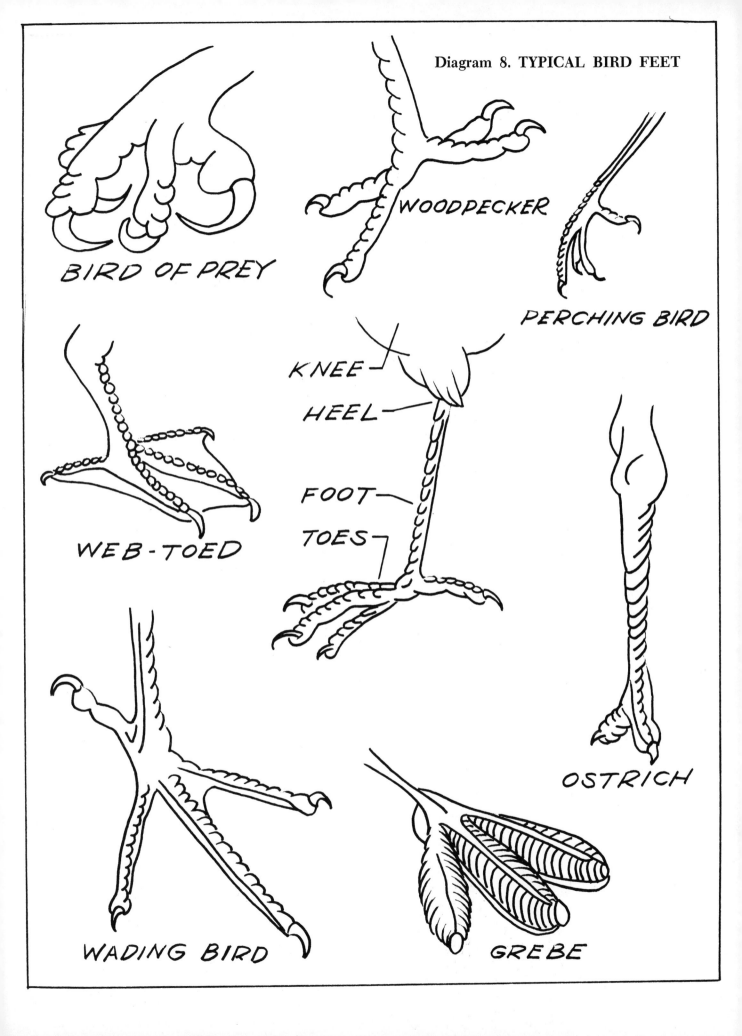

Diagram 8. TYPICAL BIRD FEET

BIRD OF PREY

WOODPECKER

PERCHING BIRD

WEB-TOED

KNEE
HEEL
FOOT
TOES

OSTRICH

WADING BIRD

GREBE

Chapter 5

BASIC BIRD FORM

When you are attempting to carve a bird, some degree of familiarity with a bird's basic exterior form will be beneficial. Shown on the next several pages are line drawings and photographs of typical birds and their basic parts such as feet, toes, bills, wings, tails, and so on. Generally, each part assumes a unique shape which has evolved from each species' major activities and eating habits. It might seem that this fact is only of interest to ornithologists, but it is also of particular interest to bird carvers. Combining the bill of a seed-eater with the wings of a bird of prey seems a rather obvious mistake, but one that could readily happen without some basic understanding of bird form.

One of the first things bird carvers should do is to obtain a field guide either from the library or local book store. Within the first several pages one will discover a line drawing similar to the one shown in Diagram 7. The picture is one that bird carvers should become familiar with as a basis for further study of bird form. As you scan through the guide note how the various species are grouped. Most guides start with loons and end with sparrows. At first glance this may seem somewhat arbitrary. Why didn't the author index them alphabetically or according to some other more recognizable grouping? The answer is really very simple. The loon is perhaps the bird that most resembles its prehistoric ancestor, and the sparrow has become the most diverse. Note the loon's feet and toes. Toes are webbed, and the feet are placed toward the rear of its body, resulting in the bird's looking unbalanced. In truth, the loon is unbalanced and as a result never walks on land. It is a fine swimmer and its feet, positioned as they are, aid in this ability. When on land the loon literally paddles itself on its belly.

The diversity in the shapes and sizes of toes, feet, bills, wings and tail came about because of different needs and activities of a species. Still, there are similarities. All birds walk on their toes, and what most people believe to be the leg is actually a long foot or perhaps more properly called the tarsus. The heel of the foot is at the visible intersection with the body or tibia. The knee joint is hidden in the bird's feathers.

Depending on whether the bird is a scratcher, climber, wader, swimmer, percher, hunter or combination of these (see Diagram 8), the size and shape of the feet differ as do the number and location of the toes (Figures 23–27). Wading birds have extremely long feet. Others such as kingfishers and scissortailed flycatchers almost never walk and therefore have rather short feet.

No bird has more than four toes on each foot, some have three, and the ostrich but two. Swifts have all four toes pointing forward. Woodpeckers (except the three-toed variety) are permanently paired with two front and two back toes. Most other species of birds have three toes pointing forward and one toe pointing backwards. For some birds, such as ducks, this back toe is almost nonexistent but nevertheless visible on the back of the foot. Owls and ospreys have the basic toe arrangement of three forward and one backward. These birds, however, can also turn one of their toes backwards thus giving them two strong gripping toes in front and two in back. This arrangement not only enables their long sharp claws to more readily grasp their prey initially while on the wing, but also to tear the flesh as it is being consumed.

On the other hand, the small nuthatch also has strong toes and sharp claws, but for a different reason, namely to enable it to creep down the trunks

Figure 24. Eagle foot

Figure 25. Long-billed curlew feet (stuffed bird)

of trees. Perchers, which are the largest bird group, have highly developed, flexible toes, the back toe being equal in length to the front middle toe. Quail, which are scratchers, have short, thick, blunt claws.

Of equal importance in the study of bird form is the bill (see Diagram 9). In general, bills are shaped to correspond to a particular species' eating habits (or is it the other way around?). Seeds, insects, worms, berries and flesh are but a few of the staples that comprise the diet of birds. Each species has therefore developed a precise instrument which allows maximum consumption of the favored food (see Diagram 10). Later in the book you will see patterns for the cardinal and the blue jay. Some carvers may be tempted to use the pattern interchangeably. After all, both birds have crests and are relatively the same size. To the casual observer one is basically red, and the other is blue; but for the carver who does not wish to paint his birds how might the two species be differentiated? Look at the bills. The cardinal is basically a seed-eater with massive bill to accommodate better this type of diet. Most of the blue jay's diet consists of insects, wild berries and sometimes, nuts. Thus its bill is somewhat long and narrow.

Go back to the field guide, this time giving special attention to the shape and size of bird bills (see Figures 28–37). Notice how the long and slender bill of the curlew turns down and that of the avocet turns up. The diet of both shore birds is somewhat similar. However, the avocet is able to scoop his food from beneath the sand while the curlew must rely mostly on the food which is on the surface.

These are but a few of the differences readily detectable when comparing bird bill shapes. It is important that this comparison be made at the outset of each bird carving. Without such a comparison, a hawk's bill could conceivably appear on an eagle carving.

Design of the tail (see Diagram 11) will also vary from one species to another. Some of the more common shapes include round (common crow), graduated (roadrunner), forked (common tern), pointed (pheasant), emarginate (pine siskin), or square (sharp-shinned hawk). The tail may serve other purposes beyond that of supporting flight. The woodpecker, for example (see Figure 38), uses his tail as a prop or almost as a third foot for added support while hammering the side of a tree. For some other species, the tail plays a prominent role during courtship. In some cases, however, it may not be the tail feathers that are being dis-

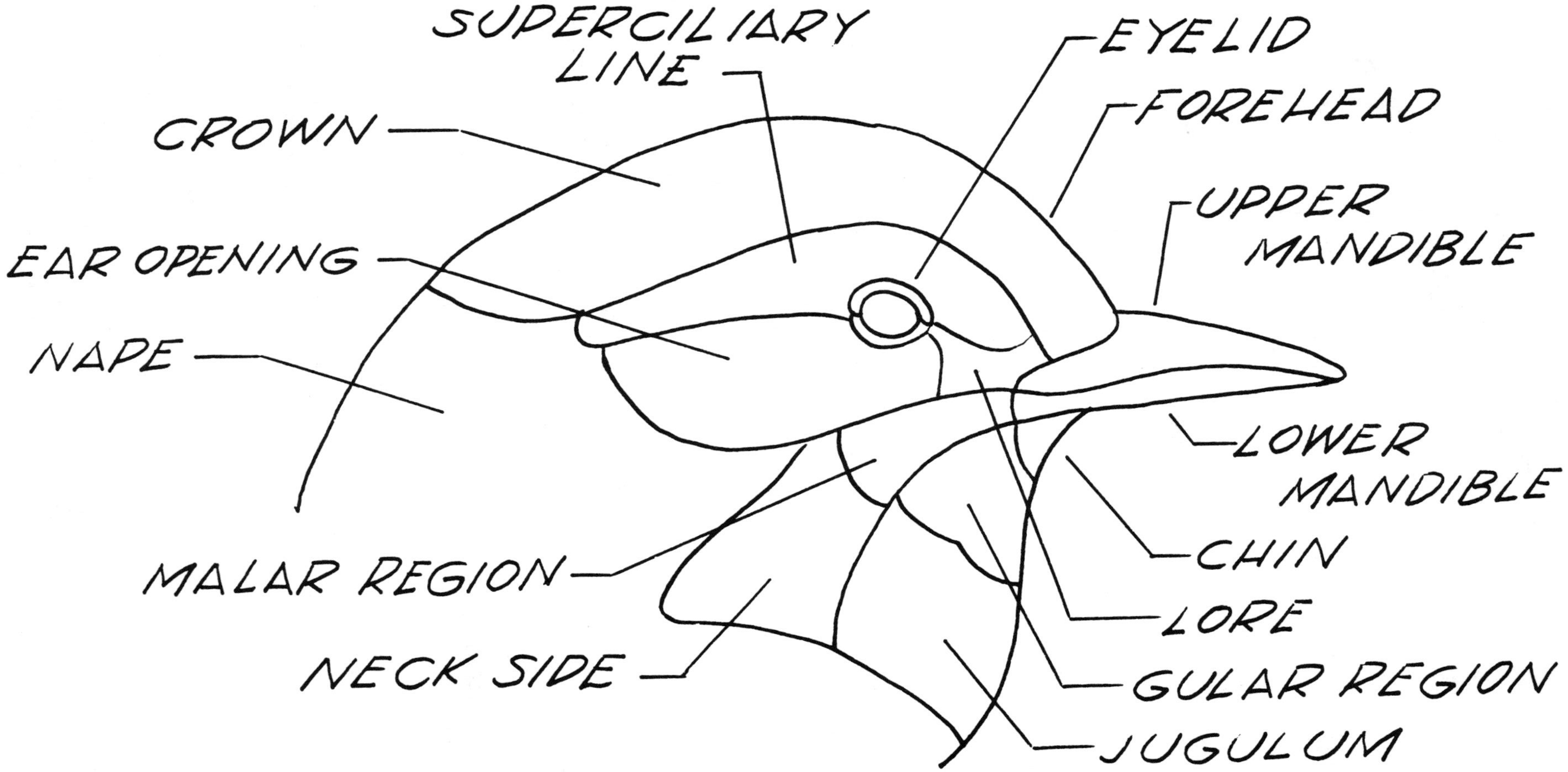

EYELID

FOREHEAD

UPPER MANDIBLE

LOWER MANDIBLE

CHIN

LORE

GULAR REGION

JUGULUM

SUPERCILIARY LINE

CROWN

EAR OPENING

NAPE

MALAR REGION

NECK SIDE

Diagram 9. HEAD AND NECK OF A TYPICAL BIRD

AMERICAN AVOCET:
SHORE FOOD

LONG-BILLED CURLEW:
SHORE FOOD

CROSSBILL:
SEEDS

GROSBEAK:
SEEDS

ROADRUNNER:
RATTLESNAKE

HUMMINGBIRD:
NECTAR

WOODPECKER:
INSECTS

RED-TAILED HAWK:
FLESH

SKIMMER:
MARINE LIFE

SPOONBILL:
MARINE LIFE

NIGHT HAWK:
INSECTS

Diagram 10. EXAMPLES OF BIRD
BILLS SHAPED FOR EAT-
ING FAVORITE FOODS

Figure 26. Chukar feet

Figure 27. King rail feet (stuffed bird)

played but, as in the case of the male Indian pea-fowl, approximately 150 upper-tail coverts.

Usually several good pictures of the species to be carved are sufficient to indicate adequately the shape and size of the tail. While the number of tail feathers may vary among species, twelve is usually a good number to carve if in doubt, especially for songbirds. Unfortunately, as in all rules there are exceptions. Some species of ducks, for example, have sixteen tail feathers; wild turkeys have eighteen tail feathers plus five more that graduate in length from covert to almost tail-size; swifts have only ten tail feathers. But if your carving is to be a closed-wing carving such as a perching or walking one, the tail feathers are usually stacked and the exact number of feathers contained will be difficult to discern when the carving is completed.

Should you wish to create an open-wing carving (see Figures 39–40) such as a bird in flight (and at some time all bird carvers will), the tail as well as the wings will be extended. Knowing the exact number of major flight feathers (see Diagram 12) becomes important. To do an aesthetic job as well as a technically accurate one you need a much greater knowledge of the external bird form. Particularly important is an understanding of how the surfaces function for various types of flight, including acceleration, normal sustained flight, soaring and landing. To capture truly a bird engaged in any of these flights will, more so than a closed-wing pose, separate the novice bird carver from the combination of advanced carver/amateur student of ornithology.

Let us compare the lifting surfaces of an airplane with those of a bird since the wings and tail of both are airfoils. An airfoil can be defined as a device of sufficient area and cross-sectional shape to cause, when in flight, the pressure upon the upper surface (see Figure 41) to be less than the pressure upon the lower surface (Figure 42), thereby creating lift. By changing the angle of attack—or perhaps more simply stated, the direction the airfoil assumes with respect to oncoming air—this pressure may be either increased or decreased. Thus, the amount of lifting force can either be raised or lowered. In addition, the lifting force may be changed by alteration of the cross-sectional contour. For the wings and tail (stabilizer) of an airplane which are normally fixed to the fuselage or body, this alteration is brought about by a combination of ailerons, flaps, spoilers and elevators. The bird has no such devices, but nature has provided it the ability to manipulate its wings and tail. Discarded wings (see Figure 43) obtained by game bird hunters will be helpful to the carver for understanding some of these manipulations.

Another fundamental difference to note when comparing the wings of bird and airplane is the method used to create the pull force or means of propulsion. For an airplane this is done by a propeller or jet engine. A bird creates this pull force by wing manipulation. This manipulation includes a combination of flapping up and down while at the same time varying the cross-sectional contour and angle of attack from the place the wings join the body to the outer tips. These changes are most no-

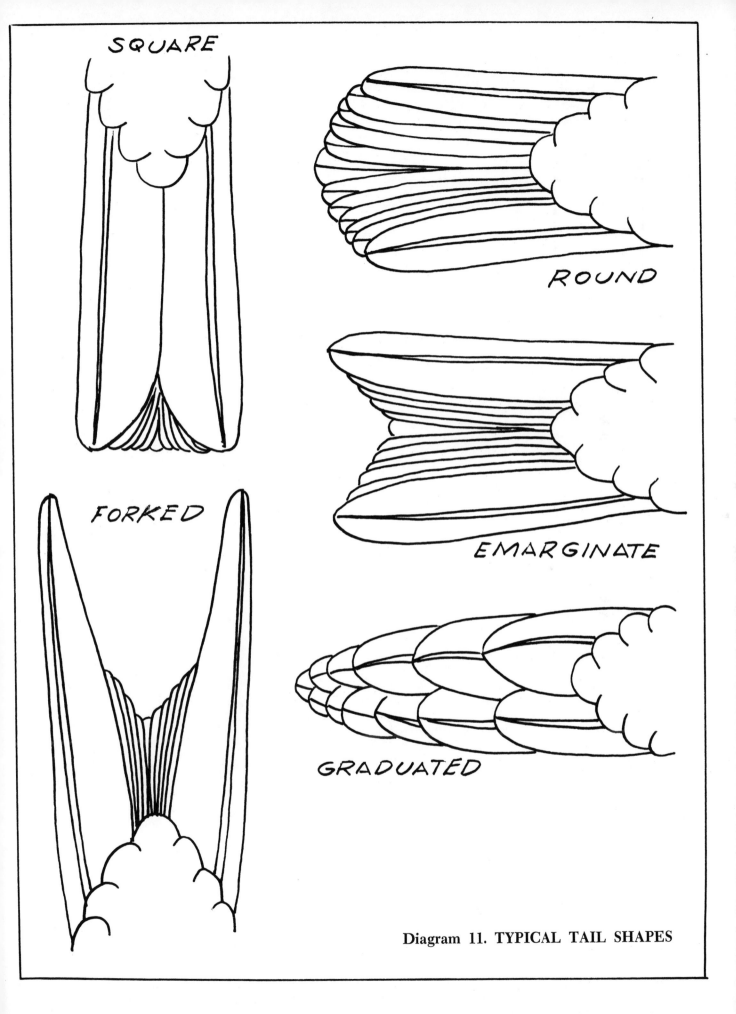

Diagram 11. TYPICAL TAIL SHAPES

Figures 28–30. Carved head and bill of a bald eagle
(top left, top right, lower left)

Figure 31. Carved head of a duck (carver unknown)

Figure 32. Carved head of a pigeon hawk

Figure 33. Bill and head of a carved kingfisher

Figure 34. Carved head of a yellow-shafted flicker

Figure 35. Stuffed purple gallinule

Figure 36. Stuffed long-bill curlew

Figure 37. Stuffed king rail

Figure 38. Woodpecker tail

ticeable when comparing such basic activity as take-off, accelerated flight, soaring and landing. The bird's tail, like the airplane's elevator, plays its part in effecting these activities, either raising or lowering, spreading or closing.

The first thing to determine before attempting an open-wing carving is what the "plan view" pattern is supposed to look like when the wing and tail are fully extended. This chore can be considerably lessened if the carving is to include only the envelope shape of these components and no attempt is to be made to duplicate feather detail. All that is needed for this type of carving is a knowledge of the nominal length dimension and the general classification the bird is grouped under.

Ordinarily birds which perform long-distance flying over the seas have long, narrow wings; birds which perform long-distance flying and soaring over land have long, broad and rounded wings; slow-flying birds of the forest and fields have short, rounded wings; birds which perform quick takeoffs and fly only short distances have rounded, concave

wings; and birds which perform swift flight have pointed, flat wings.

The tail-plan view will also vary depending on the particular species chosen for carving. Usually the tail is considered long if it is longer than the trunk, or short if it is the same length or shorter than the trunk. The rectrices, or quill feathers, are used to control the direction of flight. The termination of these rectrices at the trailing margin usually determines the tail-plan view shape. A field guide is usually all that is needed for this basic wing and tail information.

Should more than just a basic envelope shape of these surfaces be desired, the research chore will increase in proportion to the detail accuracy desired. For example, all birds have at least nine primaries (see Diagram 12) (e.g., warblers), others have ten (e.g., vireos and ducks). Secondaries range from six (hummingbirds) to forty (albatross). The number of coverts also varies from species to species, but this may be of lesser importance depending on how much a stickler for detail you are. Obviously, though, it is just as easy to carve the right number of feathers as it is to carve some other number. In order to obtain the technical characteristics of individual species, you will more than likely have to consult scientific literature. Libraries at colleges and universities that offer graduate degrees in the biological sciences with specialization in ornithology are more apt than others to have the information you desire. Some of these include:

Cornell University, Ithaca, New York   14850
Harvard University, Cambridge, Massachusetts
   02138
Louisiana State University, Baton Rouge, Louisiana
   70803
University of California, Berkeley, California   94720
University of Calfornia, Los Angeles, California
   90024
University of Florida, Gainesville, Florida   32611
University of Georgia, Athens, Georgia   30601
University of Illinois, Urbana, Illinois   61801
University of Kansas, Lawrence, Kansas   66044
University of Michigan, Ann Arbor, Michigan
   48104
University of Minnesota, Minneapolis, Minnesota
   55455
University of Toronto, Toronto, Ontario, Canada
University of Washington, Seattle, Washington
   98195
University of Wisconsin, Madison, Wisconsin   53706
Yale University, New Haven, Connecticut 06520

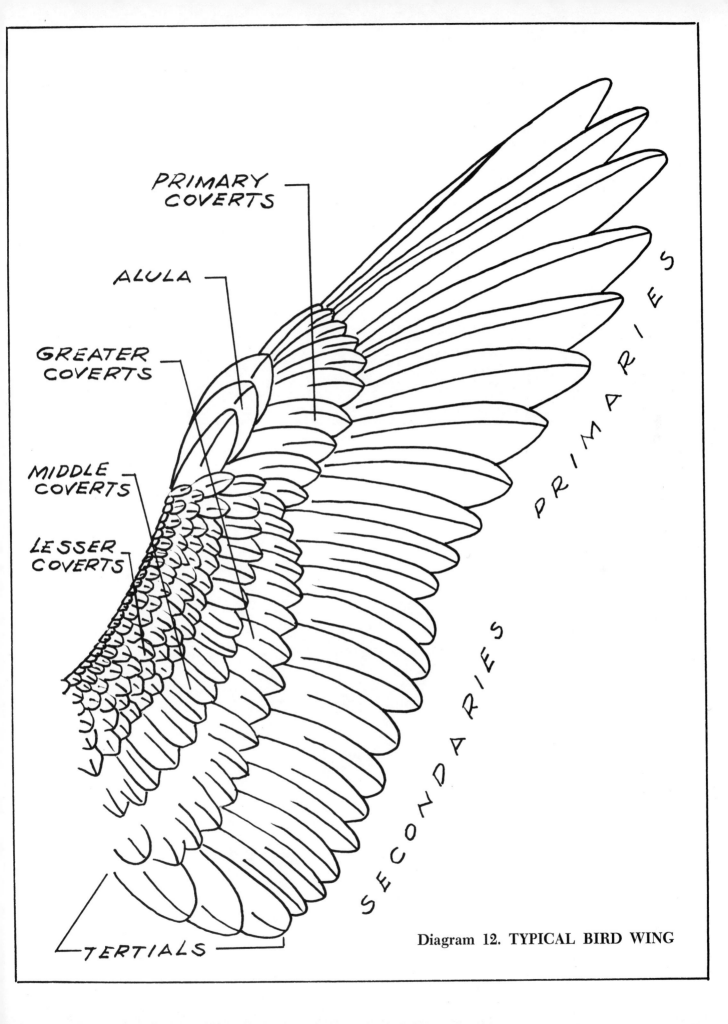

PRIMARY COVERTS

ALULA

GREATER COVERTS

MIDDLE COVERTS

LESSER COVERTS

TERTIALS

SECONDARIES

PRIMARIES

Diagram 12. TYPICAL BIRD WING

Figure 39. Open-winged American goldfinch

Figure 40. American bald eagle

Figure 41. Eagle wing, top view

Figure 42. Eagle wing, bottom view

Figure 43. Discarded wings from game birds can be helpful for establishing feather details to be carved.

Start your research at the subject index under *Aves*. Knowing the technical name of the bird will also help you get started (e.g., Bald Eagle—*Haliaéetus leucocéphalus*).

You will find that museums are a good source for specimens. While museum directors may not allow the specimens to be taken from the premises, they may be willing to let you at least count feathers. Mounted specimens are helpful in establishing contour shapes, including wing and tail orientation as assumed by the bird during a particular type of flight.

One of the most obvious and certainly least expensive things you can do to increase your basic knowledge is to be observant. Begin to *see*, not just *look at*, the birds that come into your back yard. Observe the tail, for example—is it notched or square, normally held up or down? As previously noted, collect pictures and begin to see them also.

Methods of construction vary. Some carvers will wish to make the entire bird (body, wings and tail) from one continuous block of wood. To do this requires considerable skill since you will be carving cross-grain. A simpler method is to make each wing slotted into the body from a separate piece of wood. While this will not totally eliminate cross-grained carving, it will tend to reduce it. The open-wing eagle pictured in Figure 40 was done in this manner.

Another method is to make the primaries, secondaries and covert areas from separate pieces of wood ultimately joined or laminated together. You will be wise to keep in mind the orientation the wood grain will ultimately have to assume during pattern development. As a result, one of the techniques mentioned may become the more obvious solution. One additional item worthy of mention is the time required to make an open-wing carving. An open-wing carving will take three times as long as a closed-wing carving, and require three times the patience.

The average person viewing your completed carving probably doesn't care whether you have included the correct number of primaries, tail feathers or indeed how much time it took to research the information. However, you will know, and at times you will prove to be your own harshest critic.

Chapter 6

MAKING YOUR OWN PATTERNS

A file of pictures of birds, we have said, is useful when you are painting your carvings; but it is imperative, if you wish to make your own patterns. While color photographs are preferable, black and white ones will also prove useful for pattern making. Possible sources for good photographs are the National Geographic Society, the National Wildlife Federation and the Audubon Society. Paintings and drawings may or may not be helpful, depending on how accurate the artist was in capturing details of his subject. Good line drawings may be found in children's books, even in inexpensive coloring books produced by some of the organizations listed above. Whenever possible clip and file pictures of species you wish to carve now, as well as those you have no current intention of carving. They may be useful in the future.

Ideally, to develop your own pattern, one should have pictures of the same species showing straight-on front, top and side views. Unfortunately for bird carvers, photographers and artists usually don't depict these views in their pictures—they just aren't artistic. Nevertheless, search until you find one good side-view photograph. Trace or copy this picture, including as much detail as the photograph will allow.

Next, locate a field guide which includes the average length of each bird. Be careful here. Look in the front of the guide to see which method the author has used for determining length. In some field guides, this dimension is obtained by placing a dead specimen on its back and measuring the length from beak to tail. This dimension will be too great for your purpose; after all, you plan to carve a bird that looks alive—not dead! So, make sure the length dimension is for a living or perching specimen. Also the field guide will probably tell you that the dimensions contained are average plus or minus a

certain amount (say, an inch or so) or a per cent. You'll be wise if you take the smaller length for your pattern making. A carving that turns out a little smaller than the actual bird will look much better than one that is larger. For example, if the book says the average bird is 10 ± 1 inches, a nine-inch finished carving will look more realistic than an 11-inch carving.

Go back to your tracing and either enlarge or reduce it by means of the method of squares (see Diagram 13) or a pantograph. From the drawing you have now made, trace the envelope line to a piece of cardboard. Using a sharp pointed knife, cut the cardboard on the envelope line (see Figure 44), thereby producing two silhouettes or template patterns (Figure 45). The real guesswork comes in determining the top view, if you do not have a good photograph depicting this view. One means of overcoming this deficiency is to assume that the maximum width of the bird will be about the same as the maximum back-to-breast dimension. This is probably a reasonable assumption especially for a standing bird; however, it may not be valid for a bird that is perching, stretching or sitting over a nest. Some areas will just naturally sag (as proof, observe your own abdomen while in similar positions). Therefore, it may be desirable to alter the basic width assumption, depending on how the bird is depicted in the side-view photograph. With this in mind, create a top-view pattern as best you can including two templates as previously described. Once your wood block is shaped into a three-dimensional object, you may find it necessary to revise some portions of your pattern. Be sure to do this, as you may wish to carve the particular species again at some future date.

The most obvious method for producing patterns is to scale all needed dimensions from fresh kills.

ABCDEFGHIJKLM

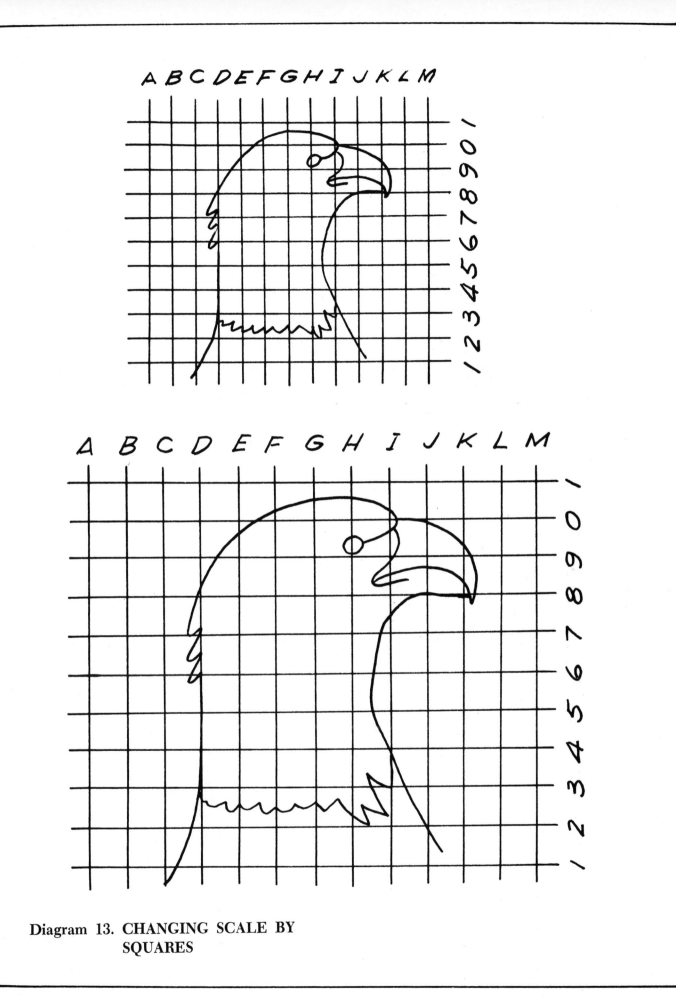

Diagram 13. CHANGING SCALE BY
          SQUARES

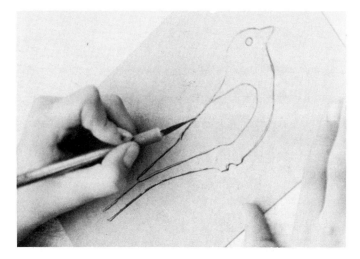

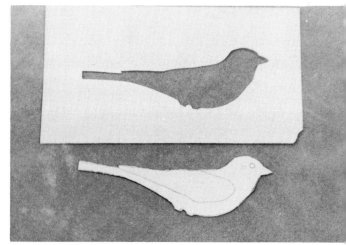

Figure 44. Trace pattern onto cardboard and cut just outside the traced line.

Figure 45. Pattern cut from cardboard

This is great for game birds but the method will not work for other birds. Should you be tempted to bag one, remember that all other birds, with the exception of courthouse pigeons, English sparrows and starlings, are usually protected.

You may not have the opportunity to study an actual bird. Thus, for study and/or photographs, a museum or wildlife refuge becomes a good source for bird specimens, especially stuffed ones. The drawback comes in your dependence on the taxidermist's accuracy. Therefore, compare your photographs of the stuffed bird with those of the live bird contained in books and magazines.

When photographing stuffed birds (see Figure 46), be sure to include, somewhere in your field of view, a scale (a six-inch segment from a yardstick will do). The scale aids one in determining what length to make the tail, beak, feet, and so on. In addition, photographs made at different distances from the specimen will differ in subject size. Thus the scale will be necessary for comparing the dimensions of one view against another during pattern making.

Figure 46. Side view of stuffed purple gallinule photographed at a wildlife refuge; note scale included in picture.

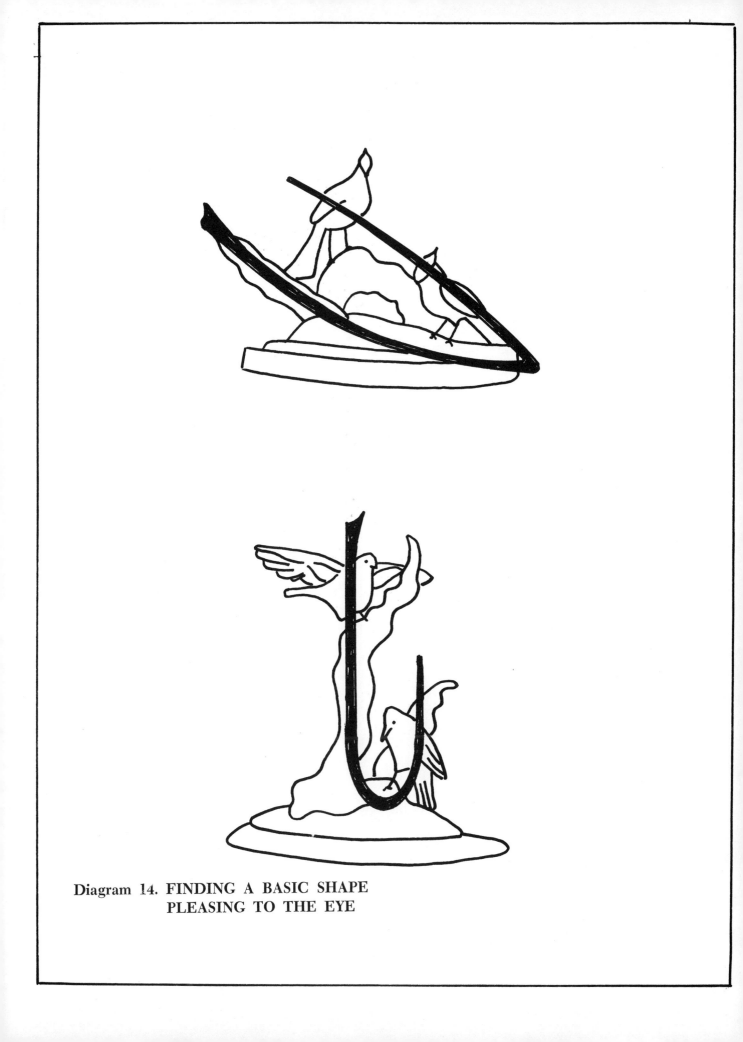

Diagram 14. FINDING A BASIC SHAPE
PLEASING TO THE EYE

Chapter 7

BASES FOR MOUNTING

Bases for mounting carved birds have one similarity to frames used for pictures. The first thing the viewer should see is the picture, not the frame. The frame may be necessary to enhance and possibly provide protection to the picture—but that is all. In like manner, the base for your bird should enhance your carving, not dominate it. In addition, it should provide stability, both from an aesthetic and from a practical point of view. Many bird carvers tend to emulate ceramic bird settings by including in their bases carved ornaments such as flowers, other foliage, butterflies and/or crawling things. This is all right, provided the additional carving enhances but does not overpower the bird. Do not leave the viewer wondering what he is supposed to look at—the bird, the bugs or the base upon which it all rests.

Another thing to remember is to keep the base in proportion to the carving. Too small a base may make the bird look as if it might topple over. Too large a base, as we said, detracts from the carving.

Do not be surprised to discover that it takes almost as long to create the right base for the right bird as it takes to create the carving. It is a good idea at least to have in mind what the base will look like at the outset of the carving. Better yet, base development should parallel the bird-carving process. This will enable you to relate the shape and form of the bird, particularly the feet, to the base material. The finished article will thus look better proportioned and coordinated. Also the base can act as a prop, especially during the painting of feathers or other bird detailing.

It is desirable to have the completed unit of bird and base conform to some general, overall basic

shape which is pleasing to the eye (see Diagram 14, Figures 47, 48). This is particularly true if more than one bird is to be placed in the setting. Settings which conform to the common shapes of triangles, crescents and convex curves are recommended. Other common shapes such as squares, straight standing or perpendicular lines and the hogarth curve (ʃ) should be left to the advanced student of design. These of course are all two-dimensional shapes. Even though you are creating a three-dimensional object, the viewer can only see one side at the time. Hence, the two-dimensional shape is what will be seen. Also there is usually a front or primary side to your setting and this is the side to which your basic shape should apply. This is not to say that the top, sides and back view should be overlooked. To plan all views concurrently becomes most confusing. Rather, once the basic front view has been established, look at all other views to make sure that they too are pleasing to the eye. It is possible and quite acceptable for these other views to assume some other basic shape than the one established by the front view. Minor modifications to the setting may be in order, however, and can usually be accomplished without major disruption of the front-view shape.

The type of material to use for bases is varied and is primarily dependent upon personal choice and the materials you have at hand. Blocks of wood, either polished or rough-cut, slabs or sections of tree trunks, tree limbs and driftwood are just a few of the materials that make excellent bases. A combination of polished wood, such as mahogany, walnut or cherry and driftwood is good base material for small song- and shorebirds. The term

Figure 47. Male (top) and female cardinals

"driftwood" is used to include all weathered wood, not just that which is tossed up from the sea. Thus, roots or branches from the forest, siding from old houses, old fence posts, or a combination of these are included. The best places to look for driftwood are lakesides, seashores, forests and mountainsides. The best time to look is during the early spring of the year following winter storms and prior to summer's layer of dense undergrowth. Never take soft wood; it it not worth the effort. Always look for the pieces that are hard. Small pieces of rotting wood can be removed, but usually a piece that is mostly soft is rotted and will continue to rot.

Do not wait until a carving is nearly completed to start looking for a suitable base. While it is possible to succeed at this, more than likely your efforts will be unsuccessful. Rather, create a bin to store the pieces you acquire, pulling them all out at the inception of each bird-carving project to check and match shape and size.

To prepare the driftwood as base material, a good wash of the piece is the first thing needed. Water, detergent, small knife or pick, scrubbing brush and wire brush will be needed for this task. Also, disinfectant and insecticide may be necessary should there be evidence of insects. Be careful not

Figure 48. Male and female American goldfinch

to remove any gray areas. Grayness is only on the surface and will disappear with continued scrubbing. Bark may still cling to the wood and although this may be attractive, it is best to remove it as it is likely to fall off in time. It will probably be necessary to create a flat or standing side to the driftwood (Figure 49). For small pieces, this can be done by placing a sheet of sandpaper on a flat surface such as a tabletop or the floor. Place the driftwood on top of the sandpaper and move it back and forward over the abrasive until it is able to stand alone. For larger pieces, locate the place on the driftwood where the bird is to be mounted. If possible, mount the bird temporarily. Carefully lower the opposite side of the driftwood into a bucket of water while holding it at the angle desired when finished. Upon removal of the driftwood from the water a tidemark will be left, indicating the location and angle for cutting with a handsaw.

You may wish to give the driftwood some color and luster. Oil stains, either penetrating or non-penetrating, are good for color while clear spray varnish or matte finish will produce the desired luster. A good substitute for the stains is shoe polish or floor wax. Another method of coloring and preserving driftwood is by the application of linseed oil. This darkens and preserves the wood but does not give a shine, which may be added afterwards with wax.

To obtain a lighter, yellow appearance, soak the wood in a bucket of water containing laundry bleach. To produce a pink appearance, soak the wood in a weak solution of oxalic acid. A soak solution of salt and water will help produce a gray appearance. Following any of these processes, wash the wood with water, then thoroughly dry it in hot sunshine. The sunshine will, incidentally, also aid in the bleaching process. You may wish to consider your mounting base complete at this point or as previously mentioned the driftwood can be placed on top of a plank of fine wood (Figure 50). This will give the final setting a more formal, completed look.

The plank may be cut with beveled edge to some standard shape such as square, rectangle, or oval, or it may be cut to conform to the general contour of the driftwood. Driftwood and plank may be held together with countersunk wood screws inserted from the bottom of the plank.

Another good type of base and one that is sometimes preferred by waterfowl carvers is a slab cut through a tree limb or tree trunk. For small-diameter limbs and trunks, a hand crosscut saw will

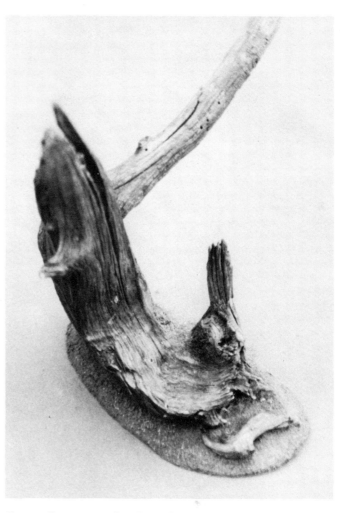

Figure 49. Driftwood and sawdust base

Figure 50. Sawdust stand in progress

Figure 51. Blue jay and stand in progress

do the job very nicely. For wood of a larger diameter, a chain saw is almost mandatory. Chain saws can usually be obtained for a nominal cost from rental establishments within the neighborhood. Be sure the wood used to make your slab is well-seasoned. Cracks and checks can be compensated for initially, but those that develop after the project is completed become an annoyance and usually distract from the overall setting.

With the slab cut to the desired thickness, remove all saw marks with coarse sandpaper. Locate a sheet of metal (an iron skillet will do) approximately the same diameter or slightly larger than the wood slab and C-clamp the two together. Place this assembly in your kitchen oven and leave for a few hours at a temperature between 150 and 200 degrees Fahrenheit. This should be sufficient to cause any remaining moisture within the slab to dissipate. The metal sheet is necessary to prevent warpage of the wood during the bakeout process. When it is cool, remove the metal and fill in with wood filler any visible cracks which may have developed on the surface of the slab. Coat the entire slab with sanding sealer (either directly as it comes from the can or tinting it with oil stain), and when dry, sand the slab smooth. Several coats of sanding sealer should be applied, sanding after each coat, to further stabilize the wood. A final coat of varnish will provide the desired finish luster.

A further type of base can be made from a sheet of stock of appropriate size and thickness, whittled down, particularly around the edges, with whittle marks shown or removed after sanding (Fig. 52). A combination of oil stain and varnish may be applied to complete the base. An alternate to this for special effect is worth consideration. With whittling completed, coat the entire top surface with a liberal amount of white glue. Pour sand or sawdust over the glue and, when dry, shake off any loose particles. The sand base is ideal for shorebirds and waterfowl. The sawdust base, with a few small pieces of bark glued on, can then be painted various shades of green, brown, yellow and red and is ideal for the mounting of forest birds (Figure 54).

Figure 52. Red-headed woodpecker mounted on driftwood and walnut base

Figure 53. Ornaments such as the carved lizard should enhance the final setting, not dominate it.

Figure 54. Blue jay mounted on driftwood and sawdust stand

Figure 55. Label attached to bottom side of stand

It should be noted that for any base, it is always wise to paste felt on the bottom side to avoid scratching the surface of the furniture that will be used to display your completed carving. Rubber cement is a good medium to affix the felt to the base. You may wish to attach a label to the bottom of the base denoting the name of the species plus other information such as habitat (Figure 55). The information may be typed on white bond paper and will serve as a handy factual reference when showing your carvings to others. Be sure to spray over the typed letters with varnish or other fixative to keep the letters from smearing.

These are but a few of many possible ways to make mounting bases. The challenge begins when you combine one or more of the methods described. Keep in mind, however, that the bird is the focal point of the finished work, not the base to which it is mounted (Figure 53).

Chapter 8

ADDITIONAL PATTERNS AND NOTES

This chapter includes several bird patterns with about the same amount of detail as the third tanager carving described in Chapter 3. In addition, a brief description of each bird's coloration and habitat are provided which may be of value for painting and mounting the finished carving. To accomplish this end more accurately it is suggested that several pictures of each species be acquired. These pictures will be helpful as reference for acquiring the proper proportions of head, wings, tail and feet. This is especially true should you wish to change the orientation of any of these components from that which is shown on the patterns.

Since it is not possible to provide full-scale patterns for all species shown here, a scale reference has been included so that you can change the pattern to a scale of your choosing by means of the squares method.

EYES

You will note that the patterns include sizes and colors of the eyes for the various birds. For very small birds such as tanagers, the eyes may simply be nails hammered into place as previously described. For robins and larger birds, one can purchase eyes from a taxidermist.

Eyes can be made, however, from a wooden dowel rod of the appropriate diameter (see Diagram 15). Eye dimensions for birds are usually expressed in millimeters but can easily be converted into inches (1 inch equals 25.4 mm.; or about 6 mm. equal ¼ inch). Scoop out both ends of the dowel rod and paint the scooped-out area the required color. Into the center of the scooped-out area insert small flat-headed nails which have been painted black, allowing the heads to project slightly beyond the end of the dowel.

Coat both ends of the dowel with epoxy or other clear-drying, hard substances, so there is a slight convex buildup. Cut off the eyes and insert them in holes of proper size drilled into the bird's head. These holes must be drilled very carefully, concentric with and at right angles to the center line of the head. If this is not done, a cross-eyed bird may be the result. Eyelids and/or rings about the eyes can be made from wood filler as desired.

AMERICAN ROBIN

Almost everyone is familiar with the robin. The handsome thrush we may think of is in reality the namesake of the European chat thrush. English colonists were so fond of their pint-sized original that they bestowed its name on its New World look-alike. Its size, between nine and ten inches in length, is most frequently used as a base of comparison for other songbirds.

Male coloration includes gray-black back, tail, wings and head. The throat is white with dark spots. The belly is also white. The breast is rust. Female coloration is the same as the male, except duller. The brood are dull gray-black with some pink showing.

A robin's nest, about four inches in diameter, is a coarse, substantial structure of mud and grass. The nest will contain four or five blue-green eggs, each approximately 1.15 × 0.80 inches. The robin is the state bird of Connecticut, Michigan and Wisconsin.

Figure 56. Robin and brood

To construct your robin carving (see Diagram 16), make the body, wings and tail from one continuous block of wood which is 2.75 × 2.5 × 8 inches with the grain of the wood running with the tail. The head should be made from a separate piece of stock with its grain running with the beak. The head and body joint is shown by the dashed line on the pattern. Additional construction techniques for the robin are the same as described for the tanager in Chapter 3.

The outline of the brood has been provided in case you wish to include a nest containing several young as shown in Figures 56 and 57. First make the nest from a block of wood approximately four inches square and about three inches thick. Several pieces of knot-free pine shelving board may be glued together to produce the block in case you do not have a piece of stock of required dimension.

Hand-turn the block to be more or less round across the 4 × 4-inch surface. Next, whittle down the bottom edges, thereby causing the block to be generally shaped like a half sphere. You need not produce a perfectly rounded sphere, and in fact, it is probably better if you don't. Scoop out the inside of the block to produce a side-wall thickness of about 0.25 inch tapering into a 0.50-inch thickness at the bottom. Add to both interior and exterior of the nest several whittle and gouge marks in addition to those already created, to look as if it had been constructed from mud and grass. Give the nest several coats of white gesso or flat white water-base house paint. Hold the painted nest over a lighted candle to produce hues of browns, grays and black.

In nature, the brood may consist of any number up to five. For your purposes, three or four young birds are sufficient. In placing them into the nest

○ *EYES FOR SMALL BIRDS (5mm. OR LESS)*

PAINT END OF WOOD DOWEL
OR SMALL FLAT-HEAD NAIL
BLACK AND COAT SURFACE
WITH EPOXY.

EPOXY ─── DOWEL
NAIL

○ *EYES FOR LARGER BIRDS (6mm. OR MORE)*

SCOOP OUT END OF WOOD
DOWEL AND PAINT REQUIRED
EYE COLOR.

DOWEL ───

PAINT SMALL FLAT-HEAD
NAIL BLACK AND INSERT
INTO DOWEL.

NAIL ───

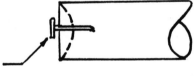

COAT END OF DOWEL WITH
EPOXY AND CUT TO
DESIRED LENGTH.

EPOXY ───

INSERT DOWEL INTO EYE
SOCKET. MAKE EYE RING
FROM WOOD PUTTY.

PUTTY ───

Diagram 15. METHODS OF MAKING
            EYES

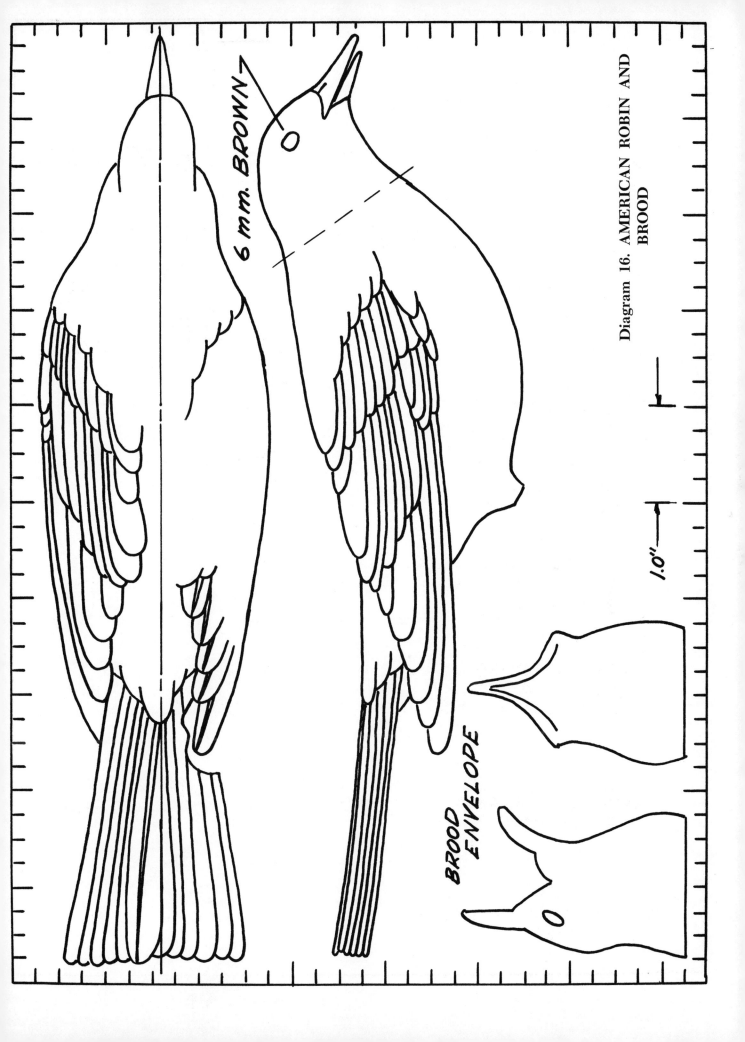

6 mm. BROWN

Diagram 16. AMERICAN ROBIN AND
BROOD

1.0"

BROOD
ENVELOPE

Figure 57. Robin and hungry brood

Figure 58. Robin's nest and brood

Figure 59. Completed male cardinal

Figure 60. Male cardinal, side view

(see Figure 58) you may find it necessary to round off the lower edges of each of the young you have carved. An alternate method is to drill the appropriate number of 1.5-inch diameter holes into the bottom of the nest about 0.125-inch deep. Should the fit not be perfect, fill in gaps as necessary with wood filler. Paint the brood as described above prior to final installation within the nest. It is suggested that a good color photograph of a female bird with young be obtained as a guide for painting. Of course a female robin would be the best but almost any songbird will do. Do not, however, use a photograph of a blue jay, since jays are naked at birth, taking some time to grow the feathers other birds are born with.

It may be necessary to flatten or perhaps hollow out the bottom side of the nest depending on how it

will be mounted. As a result some touch-up with paint of earthen color will be needed for areas where raw wood may become exposed. The nest should be fixed to its support with at least one wood screw entering the nest from the counter-sunk base side.

CARDINAL

The cardinal is a member of the grosbeak family, and the heavy red bill is noticeable in both sexes. Males are brownish red above, with breast and belly a bright red. Throat and eye areas are black. Females are brownish above, with breast and belly a yellow brown. Crest and primaries are red. The cardinal's nest is loosely made of twigs, leaves and

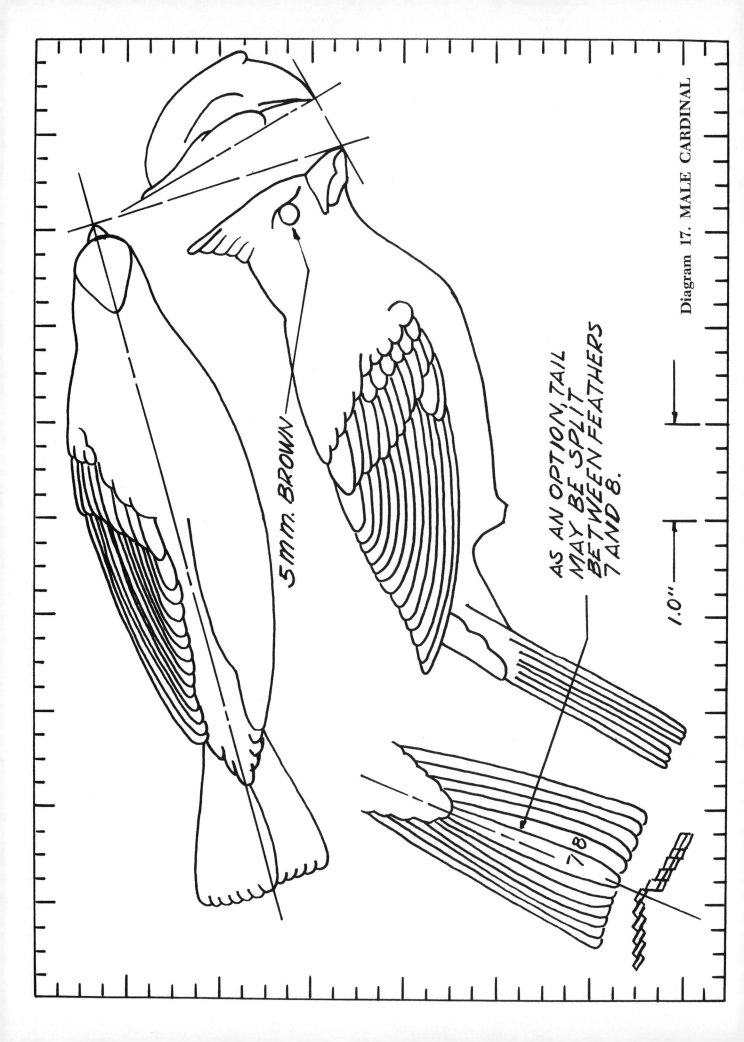

5MM. BROWN

AS AN OPTION, TAIL
MAY BE SPLIT
BETWEEN FEATHERS
7 AND 8.

7 8

1.0"

Diagram 17. MALE CARDINAL

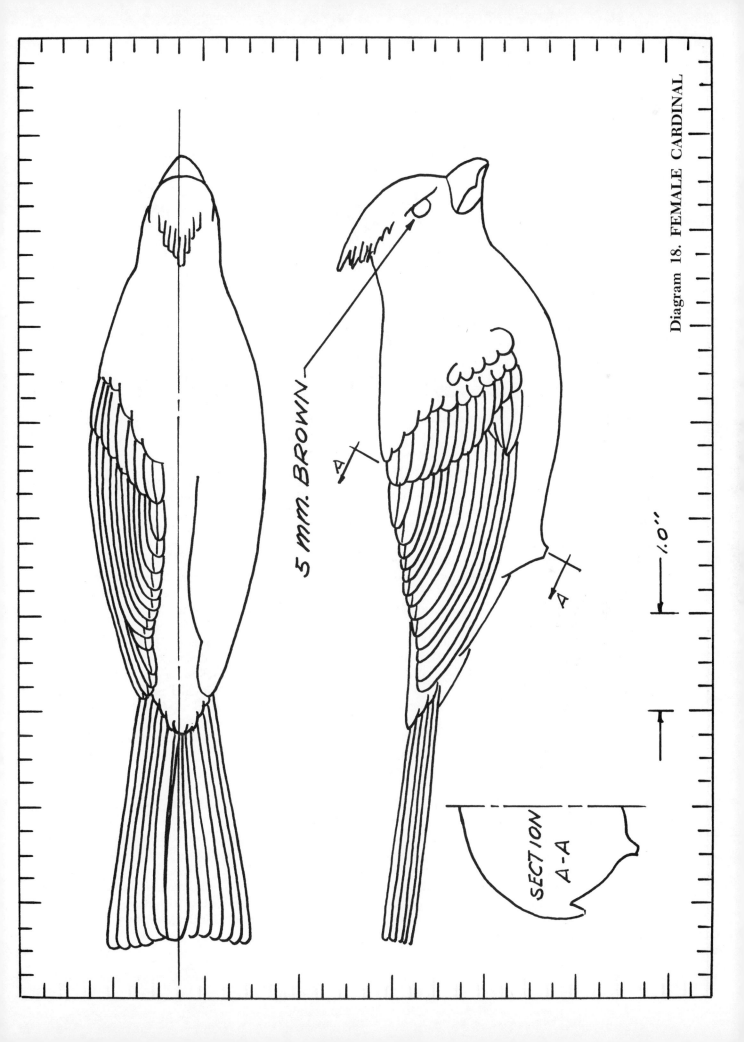

5 mm. BROWN

A

A

1.0"

SECTION A-A

Diagram 18. FEMALE CARDINAL

Figure 61. Male cardinal tail; note separation between feathers 7 and 8 as indicated in Diagram 17.

fibers that are normally placed in vine tangles or bushes. Eggs, usually four, are approximately 1.00 × 0.70 inches and are ground-color, which may be white, bluish, greenish or grayish. The eggs have spots which vary greatly in color and placement. The cardinal is the state bird of Illinois, Indiana, Kentucky, North Carolina, Ohio, Virginia and West Virginia.

Two cardinal carving patterns are included (Diagrams 17 and 18). You will note that the crest in Diagram 18 is not quite as prominent as in the other. The less prominent crest pattern should be used for a female carving, the other pattern for a male.

The female will require a block of wood 2 × 2 × 7.5 inches for the body and wings. You will need a separate piece of stock for the head. Tail and beaks should run parallel with the grain. The male requires three blocks of wood. The additional one is for the tail. The tail block should be at least 0.5 × 2.75 × 3 inches. The body block for the male is 2 × 2 × 5 inches with the grain running with the wings.

You will note in the female head pattern, the beak and crest are so oriented as to make possible one continuous grain line. For the male, however (see Figures 59–61), the beak and crest do not follow the grain line. Even so, it is possible to carve

the entire head area from one piece of stock. An alternate worth considering is to slot the head in the crest area prior to shaping and insert another piece of wood with proper grain orientation. Should you choose to do this, it is suggested that the wood to be inserted be from a harder variety than the wood previously used for the body and the tail. Carving techniques are the same as those described with the tanager patterns in Chapter 3 (see Figures 62–63).

The base shown in Figure 64 was made from two pieces of root material held together with dowels (round toothpicks) while the bottom side was cut to a flat surface. Additional methods of base construction are contained in Chapter 7. It is suggested that you scan this chapter first should you wish to include both male and female carvings in one setting.

SCISSOR-TAILED FLYCATCHER

Possibly the most graceful member of the flycatcher family, the scissor-tailed flycatcher is sometimes known as the "Texas Bird of Paradise." Its long tail, which by observation seems to vary in length from one bird to the next, is continually opened and closed as it flies, thereby giving the bird

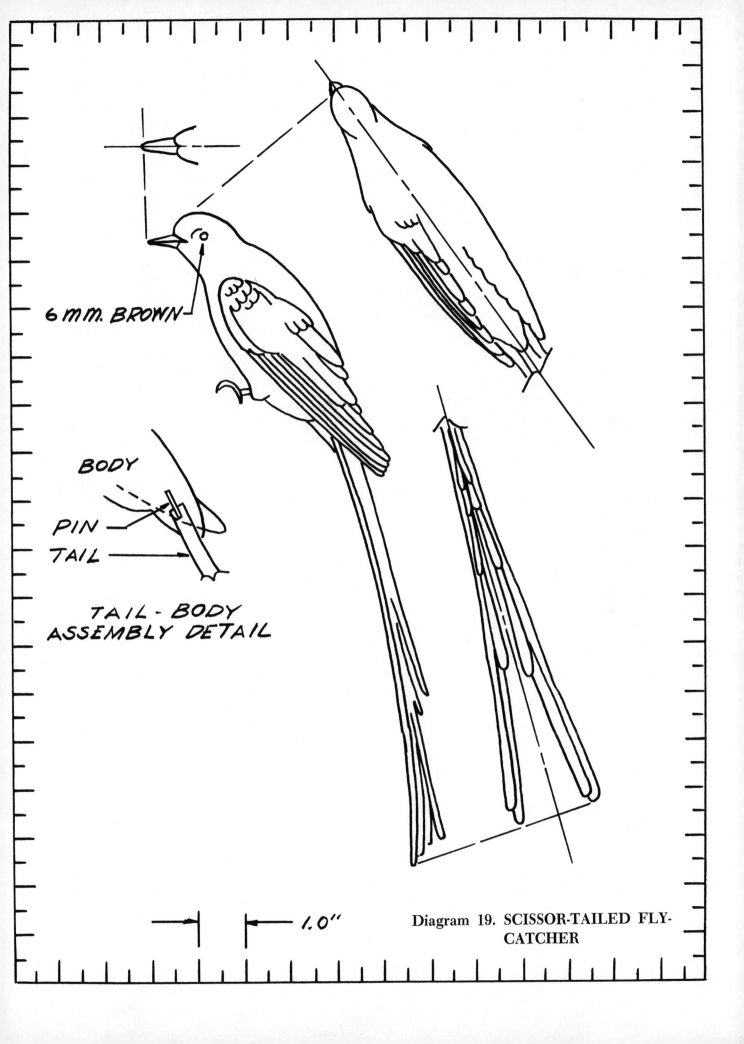

6 m.m. BROWN

BODY

PIN

TAIL

TAIL - BODY
ASSEMBLY DETAIL

1.0"

Diagram 19. SCISSOR-TAILED FLY-
CATCHER

Figure 62. Completed female cardinal

Figure 63. Carved tail of female cardinal

great maneuverability. On the ground, where the bird seldom lands, it becomes very awkward. Instead it prefers to light on tree limbs and telephone wires from which it flies in pursuit of insects, the favored food. The nest which is quite large may be placed at any height and is built of twigs, grass, paper, rags, string or other trash. The scissor-tailed fly-catcher is the state bird of Oklahoma.

To construct (see Diagram 19), make the body and wings from a block of wood which is 2 $\times$ 2 $\times$ 5 inches, with the grain of the wood running with the wings. The head should be made from a separate piece of stock (see Figure 65), with its grain running with the beak. The tail will require a third piece of stock approximately 0.75 $\times$ 4 $\times$ 8 inches, depending upon the separation you may choose between each row of feathers at the trailing margin. For additional strength you may wish to make the tail from a harder wood than that chosen for the head and body. Be sure, however, to mount the completed carving so that the base will afford

some protection to the tail feathers which will be most susceptible to accidental breakage. Tail and body joining may be accomplished as indicated on the pattern. Only the toes need to be visible in case the bird is attached to a tree limb, as shown in Figure 66. For this carving, two strands of piano wire were used to attach the body to the stand. The wire was driven through the limb and into the body immediately behind the visible toes.

Coloration includes white breast and abdomen, pink flanks and side, gray head, back and rump, black wings and black tail with some white showing. A thin pink streak should be added to the center of the forehead and crown.

BLUE JAY

Either admired or hated, this arrogant hustler is one of our best-known and most beautiful birds (see Diagram 20). Known to rob other birds of their

Figure 64. Completed female cardinal showing doweled base

eggs and nestlings, the jay's reputation just isn't too good.

Most of its food consists of insects, wild berries and nuts. Nests are made of twigs and sticks lined with available softer material. Eggs, usually four, are greenish-blue, 1.10 × 0.80 inch specked with brown.

The blue jay is found in the eastern United States and northern Canada, and west in the Dakotas, Colorado and Texas. Coloration includes blue head, back, rump, wings and tail. The wings and tail contain some areas of white. The breast and abdomen are also white (see Figures 67–69).

AMERICAN GOLDFINCH

Because of its color, the American goldfinch is sometimes referred to as a wild canary. The male is a bright yellow bird with a black cap, black wings and tail. In winter, the male more closely resembles the female and the immature, which are much duller and lack the black cap. The goldfinches' preference for thistle seeds as a food substance and their use of thistledown in nest building has resulted in their also being called "Thistle Birds." In addition to coloration, the birds can also be identified in the wild by their stubby finch bill, notched tail and wing bars.

The American goldfinch is the state bird of Iowa, New Jersey, and Washington. The life-sized bird is rather small, about 4.5 inches in length. Thus, it is sometimes possible to use scrap stock for carving a life-sized likeness. Because of the small size, the carving may prove to be more challenging in comparison to other carving projects contained herein. For one thing, there just isn't much to hold onto during the carving process, particularly if any of the feather detail as indicated by the pattern is to be incorporated. It is therefore suggested that a jig such as that described in Chapter 1 under "vises" be made in case your fingers get in the way during

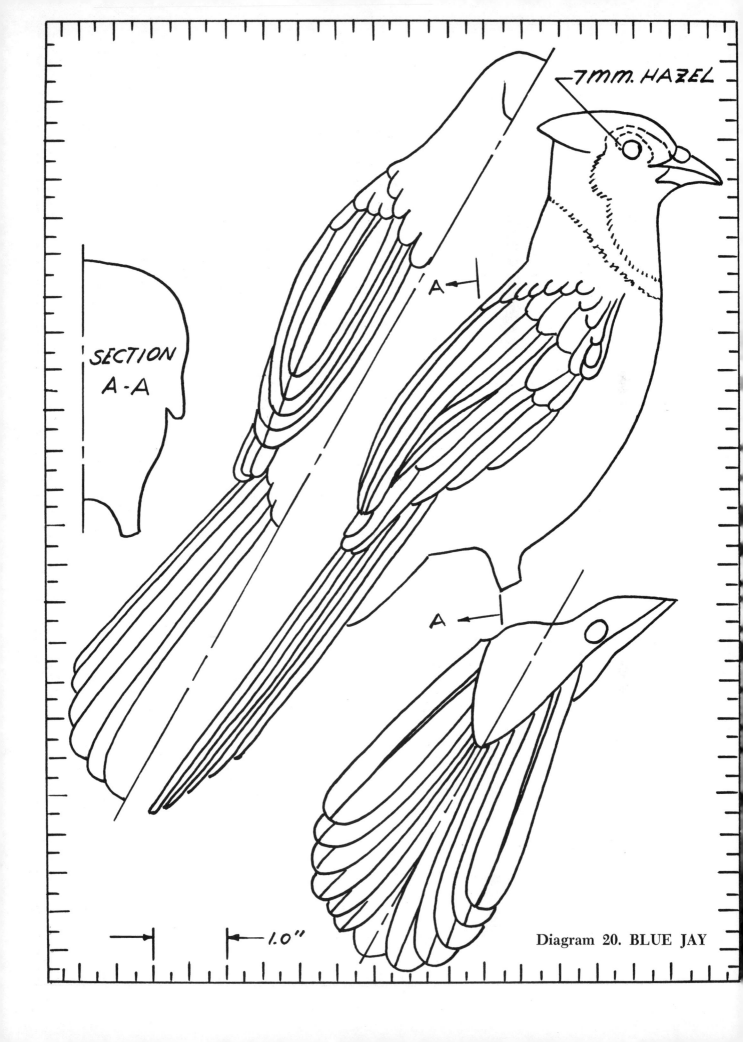

7mm. HAZEL

SECTION A-A

A←

A←

1.0"

Diagram 20. BLUE JAY

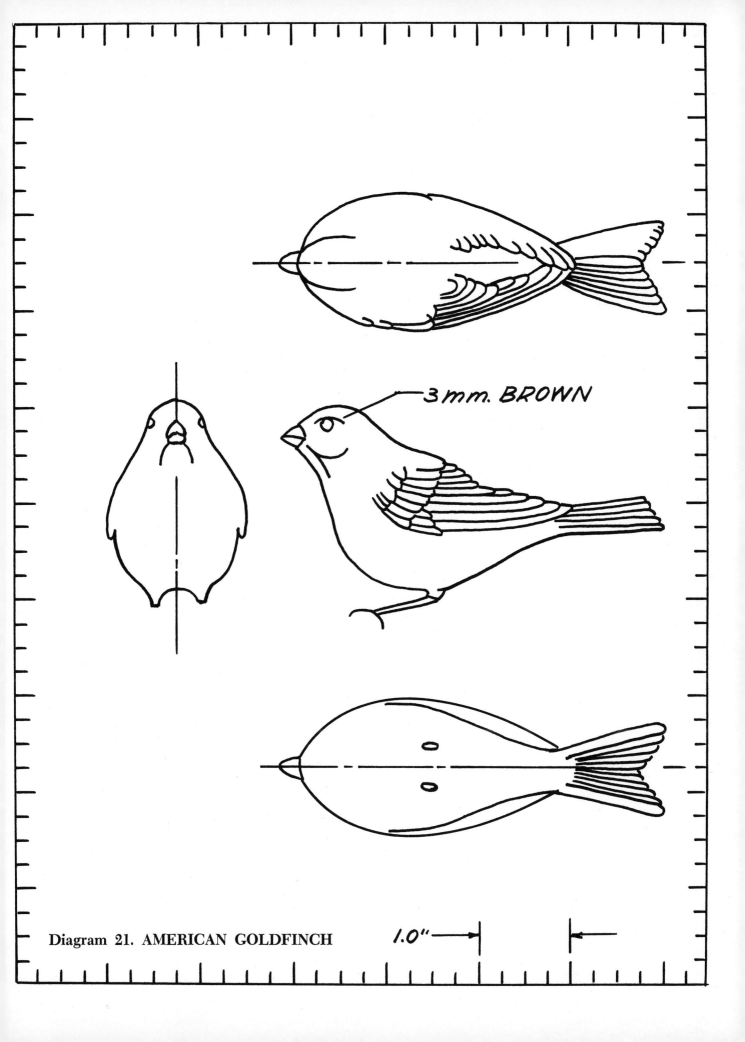

3mm. BROWN

Diagram 21. AMERICAN GOLDFINCH   1.0"

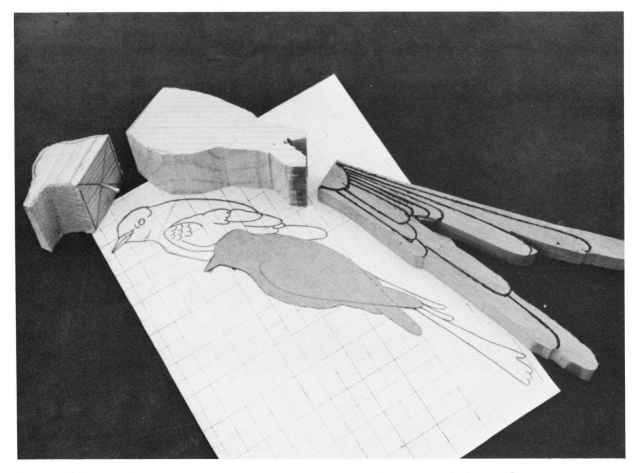

Figure 65. Carving blocks for scissor-tailed flycatcher; note pin in head for body attachment.

carving. Also, use of a clear-grained wood such as basswood is recommended for the carving block since on this type of wood one's blade will more often go where it is intended to go rather than follow some prominent grain line.

The pattern included (Diagram 21) not only produces a small bird but one that looks well-fed. Thus, this bird may best be mounted in a perching or "sitting" position, thereby eliminating the need for carving the tibia. Should you wish to carve the tibia, however, some problems may develop not previously encountered. Not only will these areas be cross-grained, they will also be extremely small. There are methods to overcome these problems. One method is to incorporate the tibia with construction of the foot. Though a simple solution, this may not totally produce the desired results. When completed, it most often looks to be just what it is; the foot was stuck directly into the body with paint

used to define the tibia. A better procedure perhaps is to drill two ¼-inch holes into the carving block at the appropriate locations, insert a wood-dowel rod of equal diameter, then shape the block including the tibia-belly area. This method works well not only for small birds but larger ones also. (For the larger birds, the dowel rod should be at least twice the diameter of tibia to be carved in order to enable sufficient material for fairing.) The main disadvantage of this method is that the dowel rod is usually one purchased at the local store and may be a different type of wood from that which was used for the body block. As a result, should feather detail be done with a wood burner, the two dissimilar woods will "burn" at a different rate, and a noticeable circular line may seem to appear between the tibia and the belly. For birds the size of the goldfinch, though, this line usually can only be detected upon the closest inspection. In case the line is prominent,

Figure 66. Completed scissor-tailed flycatcher

Figure 67. Blue jay's tail "burning" complete

Figure 68. Bottom side of carved blue jay

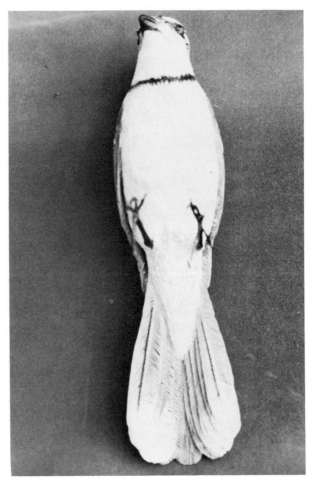

Figure 69. Completed blue jay

additional feather detailing with a knife and/or gouge will be required.

Still another method is to drill approximately 1/32-inch (instead of ¼) diameter holes and temporarily insert small nails or wire of equal diameter (see Figure 70). With these "posts" in place the tibia can be carved even though cross-grained from the basic body block without splitting away. Be very careful when removing the posts to pull them out straight, as any side load will indeed cause splitting. Similar care should be taken when inserting the feet. Remaining carving procedures are as previously described.

The completed carving (see Figures 71–74) may then be painted to resemble either a male or female American goldfinch. It may also be painted to resemble a European goldfinch, or (if it has a more slender bill) it may be colored as a pine siskin. Scaling the pattern to approximately 3.5 inches in length will produce a lesser goldfinch; and a 5.5-inch length will produce a purple finch, which incidentally is the state bird of New Hampshire. Be sure to consult a field guide for coloration of these and additional carving/painting options.

Figures 70–74. American goldfinch carving. (Facing page, top left): Goldfinch carving ready for feather detailing with wood burner; note small nails temporarily inserted at the tibia, facilitating carving of these areas without splitting the stock. (Facing page, top right): Underside of completed goldfinch carving. Remaining photographs on these two pages show the carving completed; the base is a combination of tree roots and sawdust mounted on a polished piece of birch.